# Beginners' Book

## Getting and Staying
## Sober in AA

Stories from the AA GRAPEVINE

*Other Books Published by the AA Grapevine, Inc.*

The Language of the Heart
The Best of the Grapevine, Volumes 1-3
The Home Group: Heartbeat of AA
AA Around the World
The Best of Bill
Thank You for Sharing
I Am Responsible: The Hand of AA
Emotional Sobriety — The Next Frontier
In Our Own Words: Stories of Young AAs in Recovery


In Spanish:
El Lenguage del Corazón
El Grupo Base
Lo mejor de La Viña
Lo mejor de Bill

# Beginners' Book

## Getting and Staying
## Sober in AA

### Stories from the AA GRAPEVINE

AA Grapevine, Inc.

# Preamble

Alcoholics Anonymous is a fellowship of men and women who share their experience, strength and hope with each other that they may solve their common problem and help others to recover from alcoholism.

The only requirement for membership is a desire to stop drinking. There are no dues or fees for AA membership; we are self-supporting through our own contributions.

AA is not allied with any sect, denomination, politics, organization or institution; does not wish to engage in any controversy, neither endorses nor opposes any causes. Our primary purpose is to stay sober and help other alcoholics to achieve sobriety.

## The Twelve Steps of Alcoholics Anonymous

1. We admitted we were powerless over alcohol—that our lives had become unmanageable.
2. Came to believe that a Power greater than ourselves could restore us to sanity.
3. Made a decision to turn our will and our lives over to the care of God as we understood Him.
4. Made a searching and fearless moral inventory of ourselves.
5. Admitted to God, to ourselves, and to another human being the exact nature of our wrongs.
6. Were entirely ready to have God remove all these defects of character.
7. Humbly asked Him to remove our shortcomings.
8. Made a list of all persons we had harmed and became willing to make amends to them all.
9. Made direct amends to such people wherever possible, except when to do so would injure them or others.
10. Continued to take personal inventory and when we were wrong promptly admitted it.
11. Sought through prayer and meditation to improve our conscious contact with God as we understood Him, praying only for knowledge of His will for us and the power to carry that out.
12. Having had a spiritual awakening as the result of these steps, we tried to carry this message to alcoholics, and to practice these principles in all our affairs.

---

## The Twelve Traditions of Alcoholics Anonymous

1. Our common welfare should come first; personal recovery depends upon AA unity.
2. For our group purpose there is but one ultimate authority—a loving God as He may express Himself in our group conscience. Our leaders are but trusted servants; they do not govern.
3. The only requirement for AA membership is a desire to stop drinking.
4. Each group should be autonomous except in matters affecting other groups or AA as a whole.
5. Each group has but one primary purpose—to carry its message to the alcoholic who still suffers.
6. An AA group ought never endorse, finance, or lend the AA name to any related facility or outside enterprise, lest problems of money, property, and prestige divert us from our primary purpose.
7. Every AA group ought to be fully self-supporting, declining outside contributions.
8. Alcoholics Anonymous should remain forever nonprofessional, but our service centers may employ special workers.
9. AA, as such, ought never be organized; but we may create service boards or committees directly responsible to those they serve
10. Alcoholics Anonymous has no opinion on outside issues; hence the AA name ought never be drawn into public controversy.
11. Our public relations policy is based on attraction rather than promotion; we need always maintain personal anonymity at the level of press, radio and films.
12. Anonymity is the spiritual foundation of all our traditions, ever reminding us to place principles before personalities.

# Contents

### Section 1—You Don't Have to Drink Today

### Section 2—Out of Isolation

### Section 3—Tools for Recovery

### Section 4—Experience, Strength, and Hope

# A Note to Our Readers

In this book, AA members share what helped them in early recovery—a journey sometimes full of bumps and detours but also new ideas and surprising insights. This is an ongoing process, and the results of it appear, as the Big Book says, "sometimes quickly, sometimes slowly."

"I wish for you a slow recovery," an old-timer sometimes says to a newcomer in AA. This may make some of us bristle. When we first get sober, we want to move forward quickly, not slowly. We've wasted a lot of time in our drinking days, we think, and now we're impatient to get on with our lives. We don't want to wait to get our families and jobs back, or maybe fall in love, travel, pursue some long-lost dreams.

This is not to say that eagerness for the fruits of the program isn't wonderful. Hopes and dreams for the future—even tomorrow!—help us stay sober. But we could shortchange ourselves if we hurry through these early days. We need time for healing—emotionally, physically, and spiritually. Freedom, happiness, peace of mind, a sense of usefulness, and a connection with our Higher Power are the solid rewards of taking it one day at a time.

This is where "progress not perfection" comes to our aid, a reminder that we are all works-in-progress. How fortunate that is: as members of Alcoholics Anonymous, we can continue to learn, change, and grow as long as we stay sober.

So we've found it can pay to take a moment and listen when someone with long-term sobriety says to us, "Give time time" or "I wish for you a slow recovery."

After all, sobriety is the adventure of a lifetime. And it begins the moment we ask AA for help.

—The Editors

# You Don't Have to Drink Today

*We are sure God would like us to be happy, joyous and free.*

– Alcoholics Anonymous

One way to describe an alcoholic's hitting bottom is to say it's the moment when he or she is willing to consider life without alcohol — however grim that might seem at first. When quitting drinking becomes the only alternative to continued misery, insanity, or death — that's the moment of "complete defeat" the Big Book talks about. It proves to be the beginning of an amazing journey. Surrendering to win is at the heart of AA's First Step.

Step One asks us to break through denial, admit our powerlessness over alcohol, and understand the unmanageability that our drinking has brought us. If we don't take that first drink — even when things get tough — we learn to stay sober under all conditions and develop a faith that works. Free of the tyranny of alcohol, we are free to choose a new way of living. We can go forward and find a life that's full of vitality and joy.

# —Nobody's Fault But Mine—

Forty-five, fifty miles per hour. Three police cars in tow. Lights flashing. Sirens blaring. This old truck I brought for work is perfect—for work. As a getaway car, it leaves much to be desired. I think I'm going to jail. Yet my foggy logic tells me that if I just keep on truckin' like nothing's wrong, those police officers may just give up and let me go on my merry way. (Fat chance!) At any rate, as long as I'm moving, they can't get me.

The police seem to sense that this is my intention. Soon my old truck is surrounded by screaming, blinking police cars. Together, we bump and grind and screech to a halt. I am about to discover just how angry I have made them. Two of the six officers give me a real good, up-close look at their revolvers and "strongly suggest" I exit my vehicle. I answer them with the old "Who, me?" look. They don't ask twice. One of them grabs hold of my hair and drags it out the passenger-side door. Being the obliging fellow I am, I follow my hair. Now blades of grass are poking into my eyes and a long forgotten taste from my childhood returns—the taste of dirt. I have a vague sense that the hand pressing my face to the ground is my own. From this position and in my drunken state, it is impossible to put up any sort of resistance. Nevertheless, to put it mildly, they subdue me for good measure. Cold steel is clamped on my wrists and I'm back up on my feet. Silly me, I forget to duck as I am helped into the back of a cruiser. A bolt of pain shoots through my temple and I collapse on the seat. The door slams shut behind me. Yep, I'm definitely going to jail.

I don't know it yet, but I am the fortunate one. Within the next two years, under similar circumstances, two drunks will be shot to death by police on this same stretch of highway. With those deaths in mind, I am able to look back on my own experience with a little levity and a lot of gratitude. My last drunk, the best day of my life. People raise their eyebrows when I say that, but had it not been for that horrible incident, I may never have found contented sobriety in the Fellowship of Alcoholics Anonymous. It takes what it takes, I'm told. Jail was where I needed to be at that point in my life. To the best of my knowledge, there is no good way to get there.

Those first few days in the police cells were no indication of what was about to happen to me. Miserable, yes, but oddly comforting. At least I was free to wallow in the puddle of bitterness and self-pity I had made for myself, convinced that my life was now officially worthless, equally convinced that the big, bad world was to blame for all of it.

Lucky for me, I had several weeks' convalescence before I had to face the judge. Bail was out of the question, so I was remanded to a correctional facility. That gave me much needed time to come up with a plan—a plan to get my sorry butt out of jail in the shortest possible time, with the least possible effort. I had bounced around the courthouses enough to know that the judge would not be sympathetic when I informed him that my predicament was all someone else's fault. Surely he would want to see some attempt, on my part, at rehabilitation. I would have to fake it. That meant doing the one thing I swore I'd never do again—attend AA.

I had been sentenced to AA some twelve years earlier after one of my many brushes with the law. I found those AAs to be the most sickeningly happy people I had ever met. I wanted no part of it. After all, every real drinker knows that AA meetings are nothing more than a bunch of long-faced, ex-drunks who sit around and whine about how they can't drink any longer. They just pretend to be happy to sucker guys like me into enlisting. I attended two whole meetings and left, vowing never to return. Yet there I was, twelve years later, those two capital As my only ticket out of jail. What else could I do? I went to AA.

I had many desires when I walked into that meeting, but not drinking was not one of them. I had no honorable intentions whatever. A pleasant-looking man in street clothes introduced himself to me as Murray and asked me to take a seat. The circle of twenty or so chairs were gradually occupied by inmates who looked about as miserable as I felt. I recall thinking to myself, Now this is AA. Murray opened the meeting and identified himself as an alcoholic. He didn't look to me like the kind of guy who'd ever taken a drink in his life, but who would lie about such a shameful thing?

I heard some sad stories in that room that evening—"My girlfriend ratted me out..."; "My wife put me in jail, boo hoo hoo..."—and not a single storyteller accepted responsibility for his own fate. Worst of all, I began to understand that if I were to speak my mind, it wouldn't sound a whole lot different. Suddenly, I didn't want to whine. Then came Joe's turn to share. As Joe looked up from his lap, I saw that besides Murray, he was the only non-miserable-looking person in the room. In fact, he smiled. Maybe it was just a trick of the light, but he looked—dare I say it?—radiant. When he spoke, he spoke of himself, the wrongs he had committed, his own failings, but all with the unmistakable air of hope. Hope? In this place? I hardly believed my eyes or my ears, yet there it was, of all things—hope. I began to think, I'm in a room full of strangers. What could it hurt to say just a few words? Then, when Murray asked, "Greg, would you like to share?" I ratted myself out. "My name is Greg and I'm an alcoholic." They were the first honest words to leave my lips in quite some time. Next came, "I don't get this God thing."

As AAs are wont to do, Murray gave me the Big Book definition of God, which I still remembered but didn't accept, from those two meetings years earlier. Malarkey, I thought to myself. However, after the meeting, I walked back to my dormitory feeling no ill effects. Considering I'd just sold myself out in more ways than one, I felt better than I'd expected to feel.

Then one evening, a few days before the next meeting, I was sitting on my bunk doing what I did best—pouting, stewing, blaming. Just as those self-defeating thoughts consumed my mind, another inmate tuned his radio to the local FM station. He hung the headphones on his bedpost and sat down to a game of cards. Faint and tinny, the strains of a good, old, heavy metal song wafted across the dorm and penetrated my thick skull. I began to sing along in a whisper: "Nobody's fault but mine/Nobody's fault but—"

Kapow! It hit me like a ton of irony. Nobody's fault but mine. Have you ever been in a room full of criminals, when you're the only one who gets the joke? I burst out laughing and rolled back on my bed. Nobody's fault but mine! I thought it was hilarious, but when I finally came up for air, there were twenty-one pairs of eyes looking at me like maybe I was in the wrong kind of institution. The first sane notion I'd had in years was being mistaken for insanity. I knew instantly that any explanation would be futile. Better to have them think I was crazy than to open my mouth and remove all doubt. I left them all wondering.

I wondered, too, though. It was too real to be crazy. So personal. So profound. What was it? A quirk? Happenstance? Coincidence? None of the words I knew adequately described that eureka moment. It wasn't until much later that I learned that AA's good friend Carl Jung had studied this particular kind of spiritual experience and had given it a name—synchronicity. In short, there are no coincidences. Recognizing the difference, however, requires a measure of openmindedness. Therefore, I am convinced that, had I not wondered aloud about "the God thing," I would not have been receptive to the response. The Higher Power of my understanding was given meaning that night. In my case, the god of mischief met me exactly where I was at, in a manner that I was willing and able to grasp.

As strange as it felt, things got better from that day on. Among other things, my desire to drink became a desire not to. And for some reason I couldn't begin to explain, I became unafraid to face up to the numerous charges against me. When my court date finally arrived, I stood before the judge and pleaded guilty to every single charge. I told the judge, in all sincerity, that I wanted to change the course of my life. He agreed that that was a good idea and generously sentenced me to four more months in jail, which was a far cry from the two years my lawyer had prepared me for.

That sentence gave me much-needed time to come up with a plan. Not the ulterior sort of plan I'd concocted to get out of jail, rather a plan to stay out. At the top of the list: Alcoholics Anonymous. I went back to the same meeting room I'd shunned twelve years earlier and, boy oh boy, had they changed! No longer were they the sickeningly happy bunch I remembered. Nor were they long-faced whiners. Just a good bunch of people, happy to be free and alive. I am now pleased as nonalcoholic punch to call them my home group. They have given me their wisdom. They have given me their trust. It feels good to be trusted. I try to carry the message as it was carried to me by corresponding with an inmate and whenever possible, by attending meetings at a nearby penitentiary.

As this is a living program, I have also become active in serving my community. After so many years of being a hazard, a public nuisance at best, I feel obliged to do something positive. While I expect there will always be skeptics, I'll continue to strive for respectability in my town. Miracles, it would seem, are not reserved for saints. Thanks to all you anonymous alcoholics, I'm sober and free.

*Greg N.*
*Nipawin, Saskatchewan*
*November 2003*

# —The Low-Down on a High Bottom—

I never lost a job because of drinking. I still have my marriage. I've never spent the night in jail."

When I hit my bottom, these statements were all true for me. I used them, early in sobriety, as a measuring stick, and so I determined that I was, indeed, a "high-bottom" drunk.

But, in time, as I began to work the AA program, I came to believe that my "bottom" had been lower than I'd thought. Much lower.

I discovered that my "yardstick" was irrelevant. For me, "hitting bottom" couldn't be defined in terms of externals, like my job. Rather, it had consisted of a sort of slow, catastrophic leaching away of what I can only call my soul. I have a long history of "stuffing" my negative emotions. Like so many others in AA, I grew up with a seemingly innate need to please other people: I was quiet, oh-so-polite, "nice" at any price.

At age twelve, I had an ulcerative stomach. At fourteen, I discovered the amazing curative properties of scotch and water (pilfered from my father's liquor cabinet). Looking back, I believe I drank specifically to tame my inner "lion." It worked, for awhile. I was a periodic drinker until I graduated from college. Around that time, I began to experience frightening bouts of free-floating anxiety, which I "cured" with my now daily consumption of white wine.

After graduation, I found a good job and maintained it. I married my college sweetheart. I had a few friends. But my drinking increased. Looking back, I see a young woman constantly in battle with a poor self-image. And the more I drank, the less important seemed the need for me to fight that battle.

Then, somewhere along the line, large sections of my personality began to shudder and close down. Gradually, I stopped talking to my friends. I continued to suit-up and go to work (horridly hungover, but managing to get by). I think I even continued to maintain my persona of being "nice." Deep

---

**From "Courage to Change"—March 2000**

When I was a newcomer I was one of those whom others "viewed with alarm" and so was my group. I was very young, female, dually addicted, and very, very socially unacceptable. And my group included almost every type of alcoholic that old-timers feared most: young people, addicts, people with mental illnesses, minority races, those with various belief structures or no belief at all, bikers, convicts, gays and lesbians. The amazing thing is that most of us stayed sober, despite all the dire predictions. Why? Because the two things we had in common were more important than all our differences. We were alcoholics and we believed in the program of Alcoholics Anonymous.

—Mickey H., Springville, Utah

inside, though, a profound loneliness was taking root.

Fear, isolation, resentment: these became my intimate companions. The deep inner wells, from which springs the very "self," were drying out. The walls were beginning to echo. After some time, the lonesome, hollow sounds of my own inner echoes began to grow louder than the frenetic pace of my daily, outer life.

Finally, in May 1992, I hit my personal, emotional bottom. It so happened I was alcohol-dry—abstaining, because I was pregnant with my second child. Without my shield of wine, I experienced physical withdrawal symptoms without a clue as to what they were. I felt completely, utterly alone, unconnected, dislodged, somehow, from the stream of life.

By the time I reached six months' pregnancy—still "dry"—I was enduring panic and anxiety attacks so severe that I questioned my very sanity. It surprised me to discover that insanity hurts. I wanted to die. I couldn't imagine living on and on with this fierce inner pain.

A blind phone call (and, I now believe, my Higher Power) connected me at last to a lifeline: a therapist with twenty years' sobriety. She sent me to AA after our first session. I was so sick, so frightened, so desperate, that I obeyed her. In my unhealthy imagination, I saw this therapist as a person standing on the shore—watching me bobbing, far out at sea—and connected to me by a single piece of string.

It seems that powerlessness ought to have been easy to admit, but it wasn't. Many of my early hours in therapy focused on Step One, and on dealing with the panic and anxiety.

I attended AA meetings every day. I had that eerie experience of listening to strangers describe my feelings and my drinking escapades, but still, I clung to the paper-thin belief that I was only present by default. That my "high bottom" qualified me as a "runner-up" alcoholic—not a full-blown "winner." With this came the ancillary thought: that maybe I wouldn't have to toil quite so hard in AA as some of those "low bottom" drunks.

I also had the mistaken idea that I could win a sobriety "lotto"—become sober for life, and never have to work the AA program again unless I felt like it—if only I could do all the Steps perfectly the first time around.

These illusions proved to be short-lived. As I continued in therapy, worked with an experienced sponsor, and learned a little something about humility, I gradually became aware of how much I needed AA. I didn't know how to live life on life's terms without taking a drink. I hadn't even known I was unaware of that fact.

With the help of AA's principles, its people, and my Higher Power, sometimes I now am actually able to "do the next right thing, leaving the results to God."

Today, I focus on the simple fact that I am an alcoholic. Then, I get on my knees, and I thank God for AA.

*Peggy S.*
*Houston, Texas*
*June 1996*

# —The Perfect Slip—

The day of my home group's celebration of my second AA birthday, I saved a place at the table for my sponsor, but he arrived a little late and took the last seat in the back of the room. As I started to share, I suddenly realized whom that empty chair beside me was for, and here's the story I told.

Just before reaching six months of sobriety in AA, I was having a very difficult time with a compulsion to drink. I was not sharing this with anyone and had not yet found a solution to this God problem (my prayers started with: "God, if you exist and give a damn. ..."). I decided to take a few days off to fish, an activity that usually took my mind off booze. I happened to mention to a friend that I was hungry for catfish but hadn't found a good place for them in our area. He mentioned a lake near The Dalles, and I headed up there the next day. Having failed to ask for specific directions, I could not find the lake and so took my float-tube out into the Columbia and tried for bass.

Unfortunately, I couldn't shake the fantasies about drinking and found myself thinking that my problem wasn't with drinking, it was with my actions while I drank. If I could just figure out a way to drink without hurting myself or others, it would be acceptable to me, and I could lie about it to others.

The next day, I devised a way to get drunk safely. I was in the habit of freezing ice for my cooler in a certain container, and I knew it took about twelve hours to melt. Being an ex-cop, I still had my handcuffs. The plan was to freeze my 'cuff key into the block of ice, along with a sturdy cord. I would then take my booze and beer into the woods, along with a sleeping bag and a chain, which I would fasten around a tree and padlock. Next I would climb the tree and tie the block of ice to a branch. Then I could strip down, throw everything out of reach, climb into the sleeping bag, handcuff myself to the chain, and get drunk. By the time the ice melted and the key fell I would be sober again.

I finalized my plan on a Saturday and intended to implement it the following Wednesday, the exact six-month anniversary of my sobriety. I was very sad and disheartened, but knew that I couldn't live with the constant obsessions.

The next day, for some reason, I felt compelled to go to my first Sunday morning meeting. After the meeting had started, a man came in and I could tell by the smiles and nods from the regulars that he was known but had not been around in a while.

When he was called on to speak, he stated that he was glad to see everyone again, that he had moved to The Dalles but had decided to drop by for a meeting and to see old friends.

My ears perked up when he mentioned The Dalles, especially since he looked like an outdoors type and therefore might know where the catfish lake was. I figured this might be a "God-shot" (if he existed) and I would talk to the man after the meeting.

He told about going to a meeting the night before in The Dalles, during which a good friend was celebrating six months of sobriety.

"The problem is," the man said, "my friend somehow got into a bottle between the meeting and home. Before I left to come to Portland this morning I got a phone call—my friend's young son had just found him dead in bed, apparently choked to death on his own vomit."

The urge to drink, and my well-laid plans to relapse "safely," left me at that moment, and I've never since had as strong a compulsion, nor made any other plans to get drunk.

---

**From "Admitting Powerlessness"—January 1991**

The worst result of my drinking was—and to this day is—the way I treated other people. I was young, I had ideals, and coming from an unloving alcoholic family, I had definite ideas about how I wanted to relate to other human beings. And over the progression of my disease, all this had gone out of the window: people were there to help me get drunk, they were manipulated to cover up the mess of my life, they had become mere pawns. When they became obstacles between me and the glass, they had to go. And all because I had to drink.

And then of course there were all the other aspects of unmanageability: the shame and guilt of waking up in some stranger's bed after yet another blackout, the terrible hangovers, the headaches that no pills could cure, the thirst that gallons of water could not quench, the occasional realization of the filth that I had come to live in, the increasing inability to hold down even menial jobs. In short, I lived my life in a way I did not want to, and I could not help it; it was all because I had to drink.

Listening to someone else's sharing in a meeting a few months into AA, having stayed away from the first drink a day at a time, it suddenly hit me how much pain I had suffered, how close to death I had been, what a nightmare these years had been.

When I surrendered to the fact that alcohol was greater than myself, accepted life without ever drinking again, the compulsion was removed, left me, as if it had never been there.

—Eva M., London

It is my sincere hope that some day God (he does exist for me today) reminds some suffering soul of this story. I hope he or she can go to a meeting and look for an empty chair and think about the man whose death kept me sober.

*Max W.*
*Beaverton, Oregon*
*August 1992*

# —Singleness of Purpose—

I remember my first introduction to AA. I had asked a friend at work about how she was able to stay sober, and she offered to take me to a meeting. I wasn't an alcoholic of course, but I was starting to spend a little too much money on the drugs I was now using on a daily basis. Sure I drank, but I could take it or leave it. I knew that my friend had been sober for some time. Maybe what she was doing to stay sober could help me stay off the drugs.

One Tuesday night, we opened the door to a crowded smoke-filled room. The images I remember were mostly those of older men. Everyone greeted each other warmly and many came over afterward to shake my hand. The sharing was honest and open, and I remember being impressed by that. I went to several other meetings with my friend but never felt like I belonged. I remember thinking that these people must really need all these meetings because they were lonely and they probably had no other life to fall back on. On the other hand, I still had a job, friends, and a family. And besides, alcohol wasn't my problem. I said thank you very much to my friend for her trouble, but I was not using anymore and I was sure that I could handle it from there.

For six months, I stayed clean and sober. Each day was a huge struggle. My friend would check in with me every once and a while to see how I was doing and asked me if I wanted to go to a meeting. "No thanks, I'm just fine," was my reply. Inside I was becoming more and more restless, irritable, and discontent. Then the day came. Surely after six months I'd proved that I didn't have a problem. One day I picked up and the physical compulsion returned. My disease was active again.

Two years later, I picked up the phone and called AA. I still didn't believe I was an alcoholic but I didn't know where else to turn. That night I sat in the parking lot before the meeting and I was shaking. I was no longer going into the meeting as a casual observer, but as a person in pain who needed help. I was open and willing. I remember how safe I felt in that room that night and how the things people talked about made sense to me. Being there with those people gave me the strength to make it until the next meeting.

I kept going to meetings every day, and I found myself feeling better and better. I listened to hear what people who used drugs were calling themselves. Cross-addicted seemed to be acceptable so that's what I'd say. I tried to get the word "alcoholic" out a couple of times but it just wouldn't come because I didn't believe it. I talked to a few members about how I felt and they told me that as long as I had a desire to stop drinking I belonged and that if I kept coming back, I would figure out for myself if I was an alcoholic. I did have a desire to stop drinking because I knew that alcohol would lead me back to the drugs.

Six months went by and I experienced all the stuff that goes along with early sobriety: the fears and mood swings, the physical cravings, and the relationship problems with friends, family, and coworkers. One night when I was staying over at a friend's house, I was offered a drink and I took it. I had been restless that day and the thought of a drink to relax seemed like a wonderful idea. It never even occurred to me that there would be consequences. I still didn't really believe that I was powerless over alcohol. I hadn't taken the First Step.

The minute I felt the glow of that first drink of rum I wanted more. Everyone else was sipping their drinks slowly, enjoying the conversation, while I became more and more obsessed with how I was going to get the next drink without drawing too much attention to myself. I couldn't stand the thought of sobering up before I fell asleep, so after I poured myself two more good-sized drinks, I went to bed. The next morning when I woke up I was flooded with anxiety and a sense of foreboding. The feelings were strangely similar to those I had felt a little over six months earlier on that morning I had made the call to Alcoholics Anonymous. At that moment I began to get a glimpse that I might have a problem with alcohol.

I started back to the meetings. Three months later I was let go from my job and decided that maybe I should attend a rehab program. By this time I had changed the way I was talking about my recovery. Instead of saying I'd been sober for three months, I was telling people I had been "around the program" for nine months. My denial was very strong.

The counselor I was assigned in the treatment center was an AA member with twenty years of sobriety. After listening to me talk for twenty minutes about why I was there, how I had emotions and mood swings to deal with, and how I wanted to learn to live with myself and others, she questioned me about my alcoholism. I told her I knew I couldn't drink because it would lead me back to the drugs. She told me even though I had many other issues to deal with, what I really needed to do was to work on Step One: my powerlessness over alcohol.

It was there that I wrote my first drinking history. As I went back I discovered many things that had somehow escaped my notice. The first drug I had ever picked up was alcohol. I had started drinking three to four nights a week after only a few weeks of drinking and always to get drunk. I was suspended from college because of a low grade point average, and that was directly related to my drinking. As I reviewed all the crazy, desperate, unmanageable times in my life, alcohol was always present. It had affected my life physically, emotionally, mentally, socially, academically, and spiritually. It was as if my eyes had been opened for the first time. I was powerless over alcohol and my life was unmanageable. I was an alcoholic.

When I returned from treatment and went back to meetings, I was able to stand at the podium and say, "My name is Lynn and I'm an alcoholic."

The words came freely because they were coming from my heart. I've been sober a few years now and I owe my life to AA. I'm grateful that those people I met when I first came in didn't reject me because I couldn't say I was an alcoholic. Today when I'm in a meeting and I hear somebody share that

---

**From "Living to Good Purpose"—January 1997**

I don't remember what was said in that first meeting or anyone who shared, but at the end of the meeting an attractive, well-dressed lady came up to me, introduced herself, and asked, "Do you have a problem?" Of course I said no. I was sure I had many problems, but alcoholism wasn't one of them.

The problem wasn't that I hadn't reached my bottom—I had hit it and then dragged! I was ill, homeless, unemployable, and at that point of despair in which I knew nothing would ever make life better for me. I'd been a daily drinker for about three years. I weighed eighty-five pounds, had wine sores on my arms and legs, and couldn't remember the last time I'd taken a bath, brushed my teeth, or washed my hair. I knew my life was unmanageable, I just didn't know that alcohol had brought me to this state. I thought I was mentally ill, immoral, and the victim of poor choices and bad companions. But not an alcoholic!

Within a few meetings, I began introducing myself as an alcoholic. After all, I was smart enough to figure out that was the way to be accepted in this outfit! I wasn't sure what these sober alcoholics had, but it was certainly better than what I had in my life. But I still thought I was different, that if these people had my problems, they'd drink too!

The awareness that I was an alcoholic came gradually, through identification with the stories that were shared, and through the recognition that my life was getting better. The only thing that had changed was that I wasn't drinking—and my life began to improve. I became aware that I was an alcoholic at about six months of sobriety. I was terrified. I thought that if I was alcoholic, if I was powerless over alcohol, I'd have to drink again. That fear launched me into willingness to attempt the other Steps.

What I didn't realize then was that I was beginning a lifelong process of applying these principles, one day at a time, to all of life's experiences, not perfectly but to the best of my ability.

—Mickey H., Springville, Utah

they're not sure whether or not they belong because alcohol was not their primary drug of choice, I can extend my hand and tell them that I understand. I tell them what was told to me: Keep an open mind and keep coming back, and you will find the answers for yourself. Some people stay and have the same experience that I did. Some leave and find their home in other twelve-step programs.

I believe that it is important not to dilute AA's message and that our singleness of purpose should be preserved. Many of us do have other issues to deal with and the Big Book encourages us to go for outside help in those cases, but in AA meetings, I want to hear how people are staying sober. I've been able to deal with some of those other issues by going for outside help, but without my sobriety, none of it would have been possible.

When I first came into the program, I didn't understand anything about the disease of alcoholism and how it had made my life unmanageable. I thought that people, places, and things were the real problems. It took AA members with good long-term sobriety to help me get the focus back on me. When newcomers come in talking about outside issues, it's my responsibility to keep things on track in the same loving and careful way that others used to walk me through my early sobriety.

*Lynn J.*
*Saint John, New Brunswick*
*December 1995*

# —Attitude Adjustment—

I am an alcoholic who has been sober and recovering for just over eight months now. What an incredible ride it has been. From the moment I pulled open the doors to my very first meeting, I felt something different, something good was going to happen. Those doors, which at the time I believed to be the heaviest ever made, allowed me to walk into a new way of life. I don't remember what exactly was said, nor do I remember any one person in particular, but I do remember the incredible feeling of positive power in that room. It certainly struck me hard enough to make me come back the next day, and I did. I chased that feeling from room to room, the same way I chased the seemingly wonderful effects of my first drunk. Every drunk got progressively worse. To my surprise, I found that same great feeling that I had in my first meeting in every room I went to. Sometimes more powerfully than others, sometimes the same, but never less.

It hasn't been easy. My emotional bottom came in sobriety. Everything seemed to be going wrong, with one tragic occurrence after another. My life was suffering emotionally, professionally, and spiritually. I was mired in depression. It was awful. I lost weight and was slowly losing my mind. I actually had to sit and feel all of those feelings I worked so hard to drown out with alcohol. I knew that I couldn't drink anymore. It would only make things worse. I just had to deal with those things called feelings. I guess I always had them, I just never felt them before. Too drunk to. Waking every morning, I would ask myself, What else could possibly go wrong today? I knew something would go wrong. Who knew what, but something would. Nice way to start the day, huh?

So, I made the decision to keep coming to AA. It was the only thing going right for me. I felt great when I was in a meeting. The "committee" in my head took a break when I was there. I laughed, smiled, and listened. Little by little, I got it. Then, one day, nothing went right, but nothing went wrong. It just went. I went with it. Then another day. Then another, but this time I smiled and even chuckled. The next one, I laughed. It seemed that the good feelings from the meetings were starting to carry over to the rest of my day. My days were actually getting better.

I was starting to feel joy. I was smiling on the inside. Gratitude, dare I say, was beginning to creep into my vocabulary. I shared those feeling with newcomers. I felt better. I started working the Steps and felt better still. Sobriety, I realized, is also progressive.

Now, months later, I have a great deal of respect and gratitude for my disease. Without it, I would never have found this new way of life. I have become happy, joyous, and free. Don't get me wrong: my life isn't perfect. There are many situations that I'm working to resolve, but I don't pick up a drink a day at a time. Not picking up a drink creates infinite possibilities for me. What are those possibilities? I don't know, but I do know that when I wake up in the morning I pray for what I need to get through the day sober. I also smile and say to myself, Who knows? This could be the greatest day of my life!

Nice way to start the day, huh?

*Gee*
*New York, New York*
*January 2006*

# Out of Isolation

*To watch people recover, to see them help others, to watch loneliness vanish, to see a fellowship grow up about you, to have a host of friends—this is an experience you must not miss.*
—Alcoholics Anonymous

By its very nature, alcoholism cuts off the drinker from the world. Being drunk, having hangovers, and suffering from alcoholic thinking is like being in a cocoon. For some of us, isolation—actual or imagined—was a refuge where we could drink and hang out in resentment, regret, anger, lust, and fantasies of glory, safe from the disappointments of real life. We became attached to the idea of being loners, even in a crowd, convinced that we were different from other people. We were sometimes better, sometimes worse, sometimes both—"the arrogant doormat" syndrome—but rarely a part of things.

Emerging from that cocoon, coming out of isolation, is the way we start to recover. We learn to be a part of AA by going to meetings, making a commitment to a home group, listening to other members' stories, and picking up coffee cups or saying hello to another newcomer.

Some AAs prefer sociability and people; others of us need occasional times of solitude. Some of us like to serve on committees; others prefer to do quieter acts of service. But most of us come to feel that being part of the community, the fellowship, and the program of Alcoholics Anonymous is a way to step out of the dark night of alcoholic isolation and into "the Sunlight of the Spirit." It's a good place to be.

# —What Have I Got to Lose?—

During this morning's quiet time, I started wondering if I needed to go to last night's meeting. I'm almost thirteen years sober, have some serenity in my life, am active in district and area service work, have a wonderful family and a great job. I know with certainty that I owe all of this to AA.

My wife made a promise to me early in sobriety, when I was doing what my sponsor said and going to a meeting every day, that she saw the change in me and would never ask me to stay home from a meeting. But this morning, I started wondering: Did I need to go to last night's meeting?

If I had not gone to that meeting what would have happened? Would I have drunk? Probably not. Would I have lost some degree of serenity? Probably not. Would I have quit doing service work? Probably not. Would I have lost my family or my job? Again, probably not. Then what would have happened if I had missed last night's meeting?

I would have missed Dianne, three weeks out of jail and newly sober, celebrating her fortieth "belly button" birthday with a call from her mother. I would have missed Wade and Les, driving 170 miles to the meeting because they hadn't been there for a while. I would have missed Jim talk about relapsing after twenty-eight years when he'd stopped going to meetings. I would have missed Joe realize the promise of losing the fear of economic insecurity. I would have missed Bill share how he was able to hand-make gifts for his grandchildren, something that they will always have to remember him by. I would have missed John share forty-five years of sobriety, one day at a time.

I have learned that I have only today. I can't live in yesterday, nor can I worry about tomorrow. God has given this day as a gift to me. What I do with it is my gift to him.

So I think I'll go to tonight's meeting. Maybe I'll hear West Bill share about the love of his kids. Maybe I'll hear Marty and Patty share about their three years in recovery that started with Alcoholics Anonymous being brought into their prison. Maybe I'll hear Steve, with his old Big Book, share about the wonders of a God of his understanding. Maybe I'll finally hear that new woman share for the very first time ... and I certainly don't want to miss that! Maybe I'll hear you.

And I'll be able to stay sober one more day listening to experience, strength, and hope being shared, because that's what happened when I went to last night's meeting!

*Lowell N.*
*Ashton, Idaho*
*July 2005*

# —At Home in a Home Group—

For months after I got sober, I resisted picking a home group from among the many meetings I attended. I was making a real effort to follow all suggestions, and this delinquency weighed on me. But I was scared to make a commitment.

I had excuses. In the first place, I didn't have a car or, later, a place to live, so I didn't know whether I could make it to a particular meeting consistently—never mind the fact that, thanks to the efforts of several women in the Fellowship, I arrived at the same meetings week after week without fail.

In the second place, business meetings were too much for me in my newly sober, no-pink-cloud-in-sight state. I was raw and troubled enough without finding myself in the middle of a commotion over whether to have a smoking break. How could I not attend the business meetings of my own home group?

My most important excuse for not having a home group was that I wasn't yet sure where I fit in. I was changing quickly, and I didn't seem to feel comfortable anywhere for long. Old-timers pointed out that getting a home group wasn't getting married: I could switch home groups whenever I liked. Still, I dragged my feet.

I'd been sober for nearly six months when I started working with a new sponsor. She had offered me support and smiles, several times telling me that she appreciated hearing what I had to say. It was nice to think that she knew something about me.

A couple of weeks later, she spoke at her home group, one of the largest speaker meetings in our area. I'd just passed the six-month mark. At our meetings, ninety days is the only milestone officially recognized before the first year. But six months was special to me. I well remembered being sober only six days, still convinced I'd die if I didn't drink. I'd come a long way.

My sponsor was the first speaker. It was anniversary night, and the place was full. Before telling her story, she began by talking about a sponsee of hers. She was talking about me. She called me up and gave me a six-month coin, something most people had never seen. I stood in front of more than a hundred sober drunks to take the medallion from her hand. They all clapped. I didn't dare look up, let alone say anything. As she hugged me, she said, "Don't be mad at me."

Mad at her? She'd just given me a tremendous gift. In that one night, I came a great distance toward feeling a part of the Fellowship. Until then, I'd thought of myself as a visitor at meetings. I questioned whether I deserved sobriety and its early rewards. Hearing the applause of so many strangers changed me. It wasn't "me" and "you" anymore. It was "we" and "us."

I've joined my sponsor in making that meeting my home group, and most of those hundred drunks are no longer strangers. We recently celebrated our group's 55th anniversary. I was thrilled to be a part of the preparations. With my higher power at my side, I attend our business meetings—commotion and all—and go out on speaking commitments to other groups.

Being a member of a home group is helping me learn how to have sober relationships. When I first started coming around, I stuck with the women so closely that I wouldn't even speak to men at meetings. Most of them reminded me too much of people who'd hurt me before I got sober. Now, a few of the men in my home group are gradually beginning to win my trust.

One of those men is the chairperson of our meeting. We disagree on everything possible—in the Fellowship and out—but we're developing a loving, supportive friendship nonetheless. I've only found the courage and willingness to do that by seeing him week after week in the place that I call home.

My drinking career was all about running away. I could pack up and vanish in a flash. Now, I can make commitments and become a part of something. I can let myself belong. Those actions have my greatest fears and deepest longings wrapped up in them. But I'm taking the risk to stick around, to just show up and see what happens.

*Kelly L.*
*Kingston, New York*
*May 1997*

# —Carry the Message? Me?—

I still was shaking from having spoken at the meeting so I was sure I misunderstood the phone call I received when I got home. It sounded as though the caller wanted me to write down some of the things I had shared. She felt they were good examples of what Twelfth Step work was all about.

Twelfth Step work? No, I'm certain I misunderstood. She must have meant Two-Stepping, not Twelve-Stepping. I've been in AA long enough to know that Twelfth Step work is better left to the "healthy" members of our Fellowship—you know, the ones who truly have had a spiritual awakening as a result of these Steps, not someone as "sick as I." I've never talked about a spiritual awakening in my life. In fact, I don't think I even know what a spiritual awakening is. All I did at the meeting was finally begin to get honest with myself. As simply and as honestly as I could, I admitted to the group where I was that night. I admitted that I was scared I might pick up. That I was so full of self-centered fear I thought it was going to kill me. That I was tired of pretending how far I had come in recovery. That a big part of me was

**From "So You Think You're Different?"—December 2006**

A young newcomer in my home group recently told one of our old-timers that he felt different because of his age. The old-timer's response made it easy for our young friend to stay with us:

"We all feel different. Someone here is the tallest, and someone is the shortest. Someone has the most education, and someone has the least, and both feel different. Someone has the darkest skin, and someone's hometown is farther away than anyone else's, and that person feels different because of his or her accent.

"Someone has spent a lot of time in jail, and some have never been arrested, and both feel different. Some of us don't know one or both of our parents, and some come from huge families, and both groups feel different because they never felt special.

"Someone was abused as a child, and someone else abused a child, and both feel certain they are different. Someone recently declared bankruptcy, and someone else has more money than he knows what to do with. Both are certain that they are different because of money.

"Someone has retired and has time on his hands; some single mom works two jobs and raises children and, boy, do they feel different.

"The one thing that all alcoholics have in common is that we're all different! That's what makes us so interesting.

"Personally, I was glad when you showed up, because I'm tired of being the youngest guy in the room."

The newcomer laughed. Our old-timer is at least fifty-five. It's a joy watching them develop a friendship. As the Big Book says:

"We are people who normally would not mix. But there exists among us a fellowship, a friendliness, and an understanding which is indescribably wonderful."

—Scott L., Nashville, Tennessee

still every bit as sick as it was when I first walked into AA. And finally, that I, "cool, calm, controlled" Andy, felt powerless to change any of this. Yes, that was all I did, and that certainly was not a spiritual awakening, was it?

As far as carrying this message to alcoholics was concerned, that was better left to those who really understand this program, those who always seem to have their balance. You know who they are: the people who keep you coming to meetings and praying that they'll share their experience, strength, and hope so that you can take home just a small piece of their wisdom.

Me? All I did was to speak from my heart, not to carry the message and help someone else but only out of desperation. In fact, I didn't even want to speak. The words just came spilling out five minutes before the end of the meeting. A lousy five more minutes and I could have carried all that garbage back home with me, to work out by myself. But I couldn't wait—noooooo. I opened my mouth and dumped it on the group, God help me. I don't even remember what I said. That couldn't be carrying the message to others, could it?

As for trying to "practice these principles in all our affairs," I am not even sure what these principles are. Is there a list of them somewhere I haven't seen? Hey, I'm just a drunk who doesn't want to drink anymore, and for some reason, meetings help me not drink. I am scared to death to look at myself and who I really am. But AA tells me I'm okay, just keep coming. I'm just tired of feeling alone, and with AA I can choose not to be alone. And most importantly, I'm tired of pretending that I know what's best for me, tired of letting my ego edge God out.

So, I won't drink, I'll go to meetings, and maybe I'll even ask for help. But as far as doing any Twelfth Step work, I'm not ready or able to do that yet, am I?

*Andy B.*
*Manchester, New Hampshire*
*March 2001*

# —A Dry Drunk's Last Stand—

On that particular Sunday, I was sober just about two weeks. Or rather, I hadn't had a drink since Tax Day, April 15th. I left my house at about 4:30 in the afternoon with the excuse that I was going to look for a newspaper. What I really intended to look for was an open liquor store. I'd never shopped for booze on Sunday, nor did I take notice of the fact that liquor stores in New York State are closed on Sunday. When I bought my stash, it was generally on a weekday after work, or in the morning before work. I never went to the same store at the same time of day to make my purchases, because I wanted to make sure not to be waited on by the same clerk and be labeled a drunk.

Usually, I bought a large, two-liter bottle of scotch, since that would last longer, and I was able to dispel the guilt I felt about making more frequent liquor purchases. My modus operandi was to leave the large bottle in a cardboard box in the trunk of my car, and sneak it into the house later to fill up the smaller bottles in my kitchen, basement, or wherever the liquor was kept. Being the good alcoholic that I was, hell-bent on maintaining the purity and almost sacred nature of a strong drink, I couldn't see filling up those smaller bottles with water as I've heard so many of our fellows do. That would have been, well, sacrilegious.

That whole Sunday, I was looking at the prospect of an entire lifetime of not drinking, and thus depriving myself of the only escape I knew for the pains and fears of daily living. The thought was making me cringe; it was more than I could bear. The two weeks I'd had so far were enough! Besides, I was in good health and could probably drink safely, if I were careful to moderate it this time, for many years to come. I'd worry about stopping then. Now, I had too much going on. My plan was to buy a small, pint-sized bottle, keep it in the trunk of my car, and take small nips, just when things got tight. In fact, I was absolutely convinced that this plan would succeed. I was overcome by a giddy excitement and was proud of my reasoning.

Since Tax Day, I had been going to scattered meetings, not bothering to get to know anyone, not sharing—just enduring and plotting my return to "the spirit world." So I really had no one to apologize to if I drank, no one to give excuses to, not a soul, except me, and I really didn't care about me. I wouldn't wish those two horrible weeks of abstinence (hardly sobriety as I now know it) on my worst enemy.

I pulled up in front of the liquor store, and an appalling sight greeted me: the gate was pulled down over the storefront and locked. All the tempting little bottles of scotch and gin in the pint-sized containers were sitting there along with the larger ones, calling to me, yet out of reach behind a glass and steel barricade. I sank down into my car seat and wondered what to do. Panic borne of desperation settled in. Should I pull away and head to the nearby all-night grocery store to buy beer, or ... or what? About three storefronts down from the liquor store, something caught my eye.

It was a phone booth. Unlike the liquor store, the phone was open, accessible. It was never closed. A feeling of disgust crept over me, as if I were being forced to do something I knew deep down was right, yet couldn't muster up the courage or the will to do. Grudgingly, I felt a sense of resignation, and, as if operating on remote control, I got out of my car and walked over to the phone booth. I remembered hearing something at the AA meetings I'd attended about using telephones and calling people—as if they cared. Everyone was wrapped up in his or her own stuff and could hardly be expected to take an interest in my welfare—the welfare of a drunk!

I fumbled through my wallet and came across the number of the woman who had gotten me to go to my first meeting. Not really knowing the "whys" of it all, I called her. I was convinced that I wouldn't let her change my mind; I was going to get alcohol somewhere. Half-heartedly, I thought I would give this "phone thing" a shot. Much to my relief, she didn't preach to me about the evils of drinking, or the consequences. I felt a good connection with this person, as if she actually understood where I was coming from and how I felt. After she patiently listened to me rant about the injustices of life and how it was impossible for me to go through the rest of my life without a drink, she merely directed me to a beginner's meeting near my house that started about 7:15 that evening. "Do you think you can at least wait until the meeting is over before you buy that liquor?" she asked. I said I believed that I could.

I left the parking lot, went home, and had dinner, feeling a small sense of accomplishment and a slight ray of hope that maybe this "AA thing" could work. I was emotionally and physically drained from fighting these deeply uncomfortable feelings and cravings, and was desperate to try anything that might give me some relief. I managed to find the meeting and took my seat in the church basement.

I wasn't planning to share, only to listen and maybe find some answers to my dilemma. The meeting began with a reading of "How It Works," and I was drawn to the last part. Even today, I still recite the "ABCs" to myself during moments of confusion and unrest. It goes like this: "(a) That we were alcoholic and could not manage our own lives. (b) That probably no human power could have relieved us of our alcoholism. (c) That God could and would if He were sought."

The speaker was a woman named Rose, who kept saying how happy she was to be an alcoholic in recovery. I couldn't understand it. How could a person with such a miserable disease (I accepted the disease concept, because after all, I was certainly in dis-ease) speak of being so happy? She went on and her words made sense. I felt as if she were talking right at me. "The disease wants us dead," she said. "But not all at once, in little pieces at a time." She had such a steady calm about her and a security. I just knew that she had tread where I now stood. Then the others began to share. First the beginners, then the people with time. I noticed that I was raising my hand—just another warrior coming in from the combat zone, beaten and used up. Embarrassed though I was, I shared my exploits of the afternoon and talked about the shame I felt, and also the relief that I hadn't had a drink.

Rose responded that she was actually glad that I hadn't had a drink, too. Imagine that: A total stranger interested in the fact that I didn't buy booze that afternoon! Not only that, but the senior members of the group echoed her sentiments. As the meeting went on, I developed a feeling of calm, and I truly wanted what these people had: freedom from alcohol, the keys to a new

**from "The Portals of Service" – September 2006**

My sponsor believed in gratitude as long as it was linked to action. In fact, the most oft-quoted phrase in my home group was, "Gratitude is an action word." "Into action" meant I accepted responsibility to give back what I had freely received. The living examples I saw showed me that AA worked, and this supported another common saying heard around the tables: "If you want what I have, do what I do." I wasn't surprised to see that the dictionary definition of gratitude is "a feeling of being thankful to somebody for doing something."

Being at an appointed place on time and doing the work that was asked of me was a beginning. It was a sure cure for my self-pity, self-centeredness, self-sufficiency, and selfishness. Whether it was pouring coffee in my home group, or going on a Twelfth-Step call, I entered a new pattern of thinking; I thought not only about myself, but also about others. A picture of unity began to form. The smile from my face traveled to my heart. No matter how desolate my condition, I learned to feel grateful for the day.

I was also taught that gratitude sometimes meant a sacrifice of money, despite one's financial condition. During my first year, my purse often contained only coins. I believed I had to keep every cent for my personal needs and reasoned that when I had more money, I would put a dollar, or more, in the basket. Until I found a sponsor, this was how I thought. Dorothy made it clear that, as an act of gratitude, I could begin by putting a nickel in the basket. Exercise faith, she said, that despite my financial fear, I would have enough money to live on.

I learned two important lessons from this: 1) I was a part of AA and 2) Giving—even a small amount—encouraged me to trust in the process, and in my Higher Power.

—Phyllis H., Olympia, Washington

life. I wanted what they had and I was willing to go to any length to get it.

I attended more meetings at that group and began to get to know more and more people. I found my sponsor there, and some of the best friends in my life, people who accept me for who I really am, not what I seem to be. Now, after almost four years of sobriety, I look back upon that Sunday and realize that more than human terms are needed to explain it. You see, I didn't make a choice not to drink. I didn't make a choice to get out of my car and walk over to that phone booth. I just followed a simple suggestion and let my Higher Power take over. I could have gone to a million liquor stores with no phone booth, yet that one was placed in my path. Coincidence? No, I don't think so. I've learned since then that coincidence is just God's way of maintaining anonymity.

Now, when I look back at that evening, it is with a mix of fascination and quiet acceptance. I see it as the beginning of my spiritual journey in AA. That acceptance was the beginning of gratitude. The phone booth placed in my path is my proof of God's love for me; that he had another purpose in life for me than to die a drunk. Today I'm living my life, my journey, as a productive member of Alcoholics Anonymous.

*Steve S.*
*Douglaston, New York*
*February 2003*

# —One for the Ages—

I've never taken a legal drink. By the grace of my Higher Power and with the help of my fellow AAs I know today that I don't ever have to. I'm nearly twenty-seven in calendar years now, and almost seven years sober. At my home group meeting last night, I was reminded of one of my happiest memories: my twenty-first birthday, and how I celebrated it sober.

Somewhere around age ten, about a year before my first drink, I found a perpetual calendar and figured out that my twenty-first birthday would fall on a Saturday. I had daydreamed about throwing the party of the millennium ever since, a grand and glorious affair that would be attended by all the friends and admirers I would surely have picked up by then. That fantasy persisted until, at age nineteen, I found myself in the rooms of Alcoholics Anonymous.

I picked up a one-year chip at the age of twenty years and nine months. As my birthday approached, I wrestled with the idea of getting drunk to celebrate my adulthood, then immediately returning to AA. I rationalized that my group would love me anyway (and they would have), and told myself that it was perfectly normal to get drunk on one's twenty-first birthday. I knew that many people who get drunk never make it back, and the insanity of my behavior during my last drunk had landed me in a locked psych ward, perilously close to being involuntarily committed. But, of course, I could get sober again if I wanted to, right?

As the big day came closer, I shared openly in a meeting that I was feeling ambivalent about missing out on my chance to walk into a bar and prove my adulthood by getting legally drunk. An old playmate, whose twenty-first birthday would come just three weeks after mine, encouraged this. She wanted to be there for my birthday and have me join her in the celebration of hers.

An AA friend told me that she loved me and wanted to help me celebrate my birthday, but that could only happen if it was a sober occasion. She suggested that I let her make the birthday plans and concentrate on staying sober today. I knew that she was a much better friend than I deserved, and she certainly had what I wanted in a way that the old playmate did not, so I agreed.

At 4:00 on the afternoon of my birthday, I arrived at our meeting hall to find her there with several other AAs, all people whom I really liked and whose sobriety I respected. Mike H., the longest-sober member, said that we had to help another alcoholic as a way of showing our gratitude that my Higher Power was giving me a sober coming-of-age. So, we caravanned to the house of a newcomer he was sponsoring, a guy he said was really struggling to feel like he belonged in AA. The slightly shocked-looking fellow answered his door to find half a dozen AAs on his doorstep and nearly fainted when his sponsor instructed him to change his clothes and join us.

They took me to see a movie that was probably more appropriate for a twelve-year-old than an adult (I was dying to see it at the time), and certainly not anything this group of sober, mature adults would have chosen if they were thinking about themselves. Phone calls were made, word spread, and by the time we arrived at the restaurant for dinner, our group was over a dozen strong. We took over several tables and talked for hours. I asked to hear about their twenty-first birthdays, and I began to realize what a gift they'd given me when most of them could only say, "Holly, I don't really remember."

When I got back to my little apartment that night, I cried myself to sleep, but they were tears of gratitude and joy. That was the happiest birthday of my life, and the first time I ever felt really loved by a large group of friends. Like many alcoholics, I'd always been good at faking a sense of ease in a group, but in reality I was usually ready to jump out of my skin and get back to the comfort of my liquid self-pity. The love, friendship, and language of the heart I experienced that night cemented my desire to surrender not just to sobriety, but to the AA way of life.

Today, I understand what a gift it is that I got sober so early in my life. I try to give back by tangible acts of kindness that say "You are important" to newcomers. I want them to see that the AA way of life and the relationships we build in recovery are gifts in and of themselves, even beyond the all-important gift of staying sober one day at a time.

My friend with the birthday three weeks after mine? She e-mailed me a photo from her twenty-first a couple of days after the fact. She was passed out on the sidewalk in front of a bar. Her big brother had talked her into dyeing her hair purple. At least, she thinks it was him. She doesn't remember.

I'm still saving her a chair.

*Holly H.*
*Huntsville, Alabama*
*September 2005*

# —Centrifugal Force—

For some reason, my hand went up went up when Tom made the announcement during the break that the group was going to be taking a meeting to a hospital in Queens the next week and needed another speaker. I had been showing up at the group for a couple of months, quietly hanging around the periphery, blending into the crowd. But lately, I had begun to feel as if I was about to spin off the AA planet. I could feel the centrifugal force pulling me out toward the edges. I knew I needed to inch closer to the center, but I didn't really know how.

I had tried a week earlier to join the group officially, after an announcement had been made by the group secretary: "If you'd like to become a member of this group, please see me during the break." So I found a way to sidle up to her in the coffee line and casually asked how I could join. At that point, I was ready to sign whatever documents were necessary, pony up a down payment, or put my fingerprints in concrete. There was something going on in those AA rooms, and now that I wasn't drinking, I could see that I wasn't going to get it standing around in the shadows. Well, she looked at me and smiled, filled her cup, dumped in some milk and sugar, and said, "If you want to be a member of this group, just keep coming." I managed a smile, but quickly drifted back to the periphery, the anonymous edge.

But I did return the next week and found myself raising my hand, volunteering to travel out to Queens with somebody I didn't even know to speak at a meeting in a hospital I had never even heard of. I was alternately anxious and relieved, already thinking of excuses for why I couldn't make the commitment, yet also feeling I had just taken an irrevocable step forward.

So, Tom showed up at the appointed hour with a carful of sober alcoholics coming along for the ride. I tucked myself into the back seat and stared out the window the whole time, willing myself back to the lonely periphery.

At the hospital, we stood in a corner of a big conference room as the patients came in. My mind was in a desperate spin, searching for a way out. I went to the bathroom and threw cold water on my face. When I came out, the meeting was about to begin: Tom was reading the Preamble and making some introductory remarks. Before I had time to think about what I was going to say, Tom was announcing, "And our first speaker tonight is. . ." and hands were pushing me toward the podium.

I stood there in the bright light of the conference room, looking out at a roomful of people, wondering how in the world I had gotten there. It was a far cry from sitting in the dark in my apartment at four o'clock in the morning, drunk, listening to sad music, and scrawling incomprehensible poetry in my journal. I felt frozen. My mind was a total blank. But suddenly my voice began to work; a small chip at the edge of the ice floe I had become loosened and broke away.

"I remember once I got drunk in the afternoon and decided to run a stretch of rapids on the Housatonic River in a fiberglass canoe." I hadn't even thought about this story in ten years, but suddenly, there it was, on the tip of my tongue. "There was a quiet, shallow spot above the rapids where you could launch, and I tossed back a beer and put the canoe in the water. I could hear the rapids just a few yards away, and I could feel the draw of the water, tugging at the canoe." Standing at the podium, I shifted my weight from foot to foot. "That's when inspiration hit," I continued, "and I took a piece of cord that was attached to the back of the canoe and tied it to the belt loop of my pants. I figured if I fell out of the canoe, I could use the rope to pull it back."

In the bright light of the conference room in the hospital, staring out at a bunch of nameless drunks in hospital gowns and slippers, I described how I took a few strokes with the paddle and almost immediately was pulled into the strong current. My canoe bounced like a pinball off rocks on either side of the channel. I tried to steady it, but the canoe flipped to one side and I fell out. Luckily, I was able to grab a log at the edge of the channel and started to pull myself to shore. Meanwhile, the overturned canoe filled with water and was sucked back into the rapids. As I pulled for the shore, the rope on my pants tightened, and I was yanked along down the river like a shoe behind a truck. I was dragged under the water, over the rocks, out of control. Finally, the canoe hit a boulder at a turn in the river and lodged there, and I was able to slit the rope with the Swiss Army knife I had in my pocket. I dragged myself out of the river and sat on the rocky bank for a while. I had a few scrapes and bruises on my chest and my arms, but other than that, I was okay. So after I hauled the canoe back up to the car, I reached down under the driver's seat and pulled out the last beer. "It never occurred to me that I could have been killed," I said and sat down.

That was the end of the story. It was all I had to say. How and why that incident arose out of the darkness in that moment, I will never know, but it was the beginning. In that moment, I inched a little bit closer to AA and a little bit closer to myself. Even the car ride home from Queens was different; I was suddenly a part of things, no longer just a shadow figure pulled toward the edge by the centrifugal force of my own fears.

That was quite a number of years ago, and I have spoken at plenty of meetings of Alcoholics Anonymous since. The story I told that night is simply one among many stories of my drinking—some more gruesome, some less—that illustrate my alcoholism and my powerlessness. Yet no matter how long I am sober or how many meetings I have been to, I need constantly to inch forward, closer to the center, to avoid being thrown from the spinning wheel that is my life.

*Ames S.*
*New York, New York*
*April 2004*

# Tools for Recovery

*AA does not teach us how to handle our drinking;*
*it teaches us how to handle sobriety.*
—Anonymous, AA Grapevine, March 1975

The foundation of the AA program is the Steps and the search for the spiritual connection. But it's hard to imagine staying sober without the tools discussed in this section—among them, sponsorship, the Slogans, using the telephone, sobriety renewed a day at a time, and gratitude.

AA members sometimes say they felt as if they were left out when the manual for life was handed out. We have such a manual in the Big Book and in the resources AAs have developed and used over a history of seventy years. Here are solid tools to help us handle this new life of sobriety.

# —Tools For Life—

I grew up without tools that showed me how to live. When I was a teenager, I started getting drunk. This gave me immense relief from a lot of bad feelings and made me feel I needed only one tool: alcohol. Alcohol solved all my problems.

My friends, many of them, went on to college or into various businesses, married, and had families. Grew up. Learned how to deal with the real world. I stayed focused on drinking, which I did as often as possible, and my world got smaller and smaller. After a while, all I thought about was the next drink and where it was coming from. My relationships with other people deteriorated and disappeared. People and their reactions to my drinking were inconvenient and unpleasant anyway.

I stopped showing up for work on a daily basis and came close to losing my apartment. Drinking in a bar became too expensive and entailed talking to people, so I drank out of pint bottles of scotch while sitting in public bathroom stalls, sitting on a toilet reading the graffiti scratched onto the back of the stall door.

I felt there were two ways to solve my problems. One, kill myself. Two, somehow, magically, be rescued by kind people who would take me in and take care of me.

As it happened, I was rescued and directed to Alcoholics Anonymous. I immediately experienced the "love that has no price tag" that Bill W. talks about in the Twelfth Step essay in the "Twelve and Twelve." It wasn't what I'd expected or even wanted.

These AA people kept harping on the theme of not drinking. Nobody offered me money or a place to live. They talked about "tools of sobriety" and incessantly prescribed actions I could take, like getting a home group, asking someone to be my sponsor, or asking somebody else how they were feeling that day. I didn't feel like doing anything, and no one seemed to realize that.

I took very few suggestions and nothing changed. I continued to drink periodically and think about suicide.

About a year later, I attempted suicide by overdosing on some pills I'd been hoarding. I went into a coma, had convulsions, and finally came to on my mattress seventy-two hours later. I felt awful, but there was nothing unusual about waking up feeling awful. I was relieved I hadn't died and couldn't blame anyone for what I had done to myself.

I realized something else: I didn't know how to live without alcohol. I realized that I should go back and ask those AA people how they did it.

That began my real AA journey. One by one, AAs offered me tools I learned to use, tools that solved every problem that came along.

The first tool I acquired was "act as if." It didn't matter how I felt as long as I did something. I had it backwards all along, thinking that I had to feel like doing something before I actually did it. I started, tentatively at first, to "act my way into right thinking."

"Stay in the now," someone suggested, "in the moment, on the twenty-four hour plan. One day at a time." Whenever I am gripped by fear of an unknown future and all my projections are negative, I do what my sponsor directed me to do. I wriggle my toes and come back into the safety of the moment.

Writing down all the things I'm grateful for has been a helpful suggestion. Drinking is no longer a problem, but my thinking sure is. Writing a gratitude list puts the brakes on negative thoughts, turns me back toward the light, and helps me to see the beauty in everyday life.

Try to help somebody else, my fellow AAs suggested. So-and-so is homesick, why don't you send him a card? Turn to the person next to you at a meeting and ask how they are. Call a member of your home group and see how their job interview went. I discovered that when I stopped thinking about myself all the time, I felt better.

However, being told to find a power greater than my own thinking and greater than alcohol, a power that could solve all my problems, was the best suggestion I've received. This is the purpose of the Twelve Steps, and I was fortunate to find a sponsor who took me through the process outlined in the Big Book.

I asked how to begin and was told, "Get down on your knees in the morning when you get out of bed and say, 'Please.' Before you get into bed at night, get down on your knees again and say, 'Thank you.' Turn toward that power and ask for help whenever you feel disturbed, or afraid, the way a plant turns toward the light." I did these things and found that life could be faced, day-by-day, without a drink and with the sure knowledge that my Higher Power is here to help me through everything.

I've been fired in sobriety and offered a job I really wanted. I've fallen in love, had a good marriage, and buried my dear husband. Once I became ill, received an abundance of help, and now am completely well. Precious friends have moved away; new friends have come along. Every day I discover ways to be useful and things to be grateful for. I'm a long way from the person who thought the only solution was to destroy my life. My toolkit is full today and my cup runneth over.

*Anonymous*
*New York, New York*
*January 2006*

# —Garden-Variety Sobriety—

At the end of my drinking, the bottom I hit was both terrifying and dramatic. The accumulated wreckage of twenty-seven years of alcoholic drinking and all the "isms" that come with it looked insurmountable and hopeless. I had been hospitalized, detoxed, and placed in a treatment program that had brought me to our program. While AA made no demands on me, the treatment facility did, telling me I had to get a sponsor.

Being an alcoholic, the first thing I did was complicate the situation. My sponsor would have to be perfect in every way. After a long period of frus-

---

**From "Desperately Seeking Solutions"—April 2001**

When I was "out there," I always was looking for The Answer: the substance, the person, the place, the piece of information that would fix me, the one thing that would solve my problems and answer my questions. After sixteen years of sobriety, I realize that I now have found my answer, and it is very simple: one day at a time, I don't pick up a drink or a drug—no matter what I feel like, no matter what is happening in my life. That's it. (Oh, and going to meetings, praying, and talking to trusted advisors help a lot, too.)

—Alison E., Gill, Massachusetts

---

trated searching, I related my dilemma to an AA acquaintance. He suggested a men's "deer camp" AA group that had been meeting continuously for over thirty years. They always started that meeting the same way. The chairman said, "At this meeting, we stress sponsorship. Is there anyone who doesn't have a sponsor and would like to get one?"

I jumped up out of my chair in front of this room full of men and said, "Yes, I'd like to interview several of you about being my sponsor after the meeting." The room erupted in laughter as I stood there feeling foolish. But when the noise subsided, the chairman said to me in the most gentle way, "Well, we don't have to make it that complicated. How about if I just appoint you a sponsor?"

Embarrassed and perplexed, I told him that would be okay. Looking around the room, the chairman settled on an old man sitting off to one side. "Charlie," he said, "will you sponsor this man?"

The look Charlie gave me spoke volumes. He started to shake his head and wave me off, but suddenly he said, "Oh alright. See me after the meeting." (Later, I would learn that this is a traditional charade of these old-timers, and in time I would take to doing it myself.)

After the meeting, Charlie looked me in the eye and asked, "Are you willing to go to any lengths to get this program?" Unsure of what he intended by this, I asked what he meant. "It means," he answered, "are you willing to do whatever I ask you, with the understanding that I did it myself?" Well, if he'd done it, I could too, so I agreed to do whatever he said.

Charlie was an old-timer—seventeen years sober when we began working the program together. He sponsored me the way he'd been sponsored. Shortly after we began, he asked if I'd be willing to garden with him. I certainly wasn't enthusiastic, but I had said I'd go to any lengths, so I agreed. And so, this sober old man and I began a vegetable garden. Charlie liked to tell his friends that we were "farming" together. He showed me everything about how you plan, build, prepare, and plant a garden.

We cleared and dug and tilled and raked. It was hard work, but we did it at Charlie's pace, and it felt good. I got my hands dirty.

As we began to put in rows of plants, Charlie got down on his knees in our newly tilled earth and indicated for me to follow him. I got on my knees in the dirt, and this gentle old man looked at me with a wry smile and said, "As long as we're down here, let's say the Serenity Prayer." We said it together, and that was the first time I'd ever prayed on my knees.

Vegetable gardens need a lot of daily care. Charlie said it was necessary to pull weeds and water the plants early each morning, and at day's end when they had stood up to the blistering sun, another watering for the night's rest

---

**From "What is Acceptance?"—March 1962**

Another exercise that I practice is to try for a full inventory of my blessings and then for a right acceptance of the many gifts that are mine—both temporal and spiritual. Here I try to achieve a state of joyful gratitude. When such a brand of gratitude is repeatedly affirmed and pondered, it can finally displace the natural tendency to congratulate myself on whatever progress I may have been enabled to make in some areas of living. I try hard to hold fast to the truth that a full and thankful heart cannot entertain great conceits. When brimming with gratitude, one's heart-beat must surely result in outgoing love, the finest emotion that we can ever know.

—Bill W.

and recovery. So I showed up at our garden every morning just after sunup, and Charlie would already be there waiting for me. As we worked together in the cool morning air, I'd ramble on and on about my expectations for the coming day while he listened patiently.

When I finally wound down, Charlie would allow me to choose only one, or at most two actions for that day, and disregard the rest. These were my "marching orders," and I would return to the garden at sundown to describe how all of it had gone. Occasionally, he'd make a comment, but mostly he let me come to my own realizations as he gently steered the course. For days and months we did this together, as I slowly came into the sunlight of the spirit and the AA design for living. From our vegetable garden, we launched into the Twelve Steps.

Seven years passed this way. One morning as I answered the phones at our Central Office the way Charlie had taught me, he called and asked me to come and see him. It was two days before Thanksgiving when he looked at me and said, "Don, I've got cancer, and it's terminal."

For six months as Charlie grew weaker, he faced each day as a gift with a grateful attitude. He never spoke of himself, only of the program and the newcomer. Finally one Saturday he asked me to meet him in his garden. He wanted me to move a few plants around for him. The next day was Sunday, and they took him to the hospital in the afternoon. I got to see him Monday morning, and he was almost gone, but he said my name and he held my hand. Later that morning, my sponsor passed away.

I'll always know that Charlie called me back to the garden one last time to make sure I'd remember the lessons we learned there together and to pass them on to others. And to remind me that this sober life of ours is a miraculous gift, to be lived to the fullest one day at a time. And when it's over, to go with quiet dignity, grateful to have trudged the road of happy destiny.

*Don G.*
*Little Rock, Arkansas*
*December 2004*

# —One Brick at a Time—

"How are you, John?" my sponsor used to ask as we shook hands. As a newcomer I would think, Wow, this is great! Here's a guy who genuinely wants to know about my life. So I'd tell him: "Well, my mortgage is too high. I have the world's worst marriage. I hate my job. My in-laws treat me like an escaped killer and my car payment is killing me …." And on and on.

During those early months of my sobriety, my sponsor must have made up his mind to allow me to rant and rave for a while. And then one night I walked into his office and, as he shook my hand, he asked his standard question: "How are you, John?" Then he squeezed my hand, adding a word. "How are you, John—inside?"

Nobody had ever asked me that before. I squirmed and fidgeted. This is

---

**From "In the Beginning…"—May 1989**

One tool that helped me early in my sobriety was the slogan H.A.L.T.: Don't get too hungry, too angry, too lonely, or too tired. I had been working long hours for a ten-day period without a meeting when my boss brought in another man for me to train. I at once figured that I was on the way out and this guy was going to take over. I got angry, I hadn't eaten regularly, and I was very tired from working long hours. And I was lonely for my AA friends. Well, I did do one thing right. I phoned an AA member and immediately got help. It was suggested that I go right over to the market across the street and get some honey, orange juice, and vitamin pills, then take a quick Step Ten. I took a personal inventory and found out that I was pouting and miserable because my boss had hired that other guy. So I went to my boss and apologized. Later I found out that it was for my own good that he hired another man, because the work load was too much for me alone. Today the two of us work beautifully on this job that I tried to do all by myself. Now I have more time for AA meetings.

—Hal R., Millbrae, California

it, I thought. This is the part where I'm supposed to open up and share my inner self. But how could I tell him that I had no inner self? That, in my case, there was nobody home. If I'd been honest and open from the beginning of our relationship, I would have told him that I'd spent my entire adult life avoiding people who talked that way.

In fact, I was so uncomfortable when other people shared their feelings that when I attended my first few AA meetings, I'd hear people sharing and I'd think, Oh God. Someday that's going to be me up there. Most of the time I couldn't make it to the end of the meeting. I would get up and pretend to go to the bathroom. Then, I'd casually sneak out to the parking lot to the safety of my car.

That night in my sponsor's office he finally let go of my hand, but he still had me trapped in the chair. "Inside?" I repeated as if it were a foreign word and I wasn't really sure of its meaning. He nodded yes.

I started my recovery that night. Beginning that night, in that chair, in that office, and for many nights to come, I started opening up. What choice did I have? Each time we shook hands he asked me that same question, until, finally, he didn't have to ask it anymore. When I told him how I was, I automatically told him how I was inside.

His plan worked. Beginning with that stark, unabashed question, my sponsor helped me to tear down the walls of my resistance one brick at a time. It's been quite a while since that night in my sponsor's office. I've learned to share my inner feelings in meetings and with dozens of guys one-on-one. I've learned that my inner feelings boil down to a handful of things—fear, anger, self-pity, shame, and feelings of inadequacy and low self-esteem.

These are the things we need to talk about in AA. Forget about your car payment and your in-laws and your boss and the contractor who didn't show up. Why waste your time—and everybody else's—whining about things you can't do anything about anyway?

Consider this: long before there was the Big Book or the "Twelve and Twelve" or any literature or even any meetings, the simple principle of AA was working. It started when Bill met Dr. Bob and it's been working ever since. And there's no reason to think it won't continue to work.

What is that simple principle? One alcoholic talking with another alcoholic. One recovering alcoholic sharing with another alcoholic how he feels inside.

*John Y.*
*Russell, Pennsylvania*
*December 2004*

# —A Perfectly Practical Program—

I arrived at AA in a shattered condition. I'd lost everything I'd been taught was worth living for: wife, children, career. I already had no friends because of my incessant drive to shrink my world by sitting in a chair in my living room and drinking alone, night after lonely night.

Finding that there was nowhere left to hide after a blackout (which resulted in a fire in that chair), I was accompanied to my first meeting by Ray. Ray was then seventeen years sober and from the look of him certainly needed AA. After he'd spent several weeks shepherding me to meetings, I managed to drive him away with my less than friendly temperament and proceeded to do it my way—alone. I trudged desperately from one meeting to another, knowing I couldn't drink. In between I retreated to that fire-scarred chair and sat, alone, alone, alone until it was time for the next meeting. I kept going to AA because there was no place else, but I kept myself isolated from the people in AA. At every meeting I attended I sat by myself, away from the group, uninvolved, like a frightened animal. I felt superior to all those drunks.

Six months into this I was at another bottom. My life was a mess practically and emotionally, and though I'd not yet picked up a drink, I was still alone and desperate. I couldn't take it anymore.

That's when I found the courage to ask Al for help. He was sober ten years, active in AA, and had a positive attitude. Al brought me to different meetings,

---

**From "Old Advice"—August 2000**

"Keep it simple," Toni said. It was after a morning AA meeting where I'd once again found myself questioning the purpose of life, or, more pointedly, my place in it. "Listen," she said, "you're a good man. You're a good father, a good husband, a good member of this group and this community. What more do you need?" She wasn't taking my inventory. She was reminding me to have some gratitude and to change my perspective.

"Focus on what you have," she said.

It was old advice. I'd heard it many times in my fifteen years in AA. But this morning, hearing it from an old friend and a member of my home group who was looking me straight in the eye—that was something new.

For an instant I experienced what Bill W. might have felt after his final meeting with Dr. Bob, when Dr. Bob said, "Let's not louse this thing up. Let's keep it simple." I always thought that Dr. Bob was talking about the future of Alcoholics Anonymous. But now I think that the "it" he wanted to keep simple also referred to "life," more specifically the life of every single member of AA. And that includes me.

That's what Toni was saying: you've got one life to live. Don't screw it up with a lot of maybes, what-ifs, and could-have-beens. Focus on what you have.

—Wally L., Carmel Valley, California

---

away from the clubhouse group where I'd hidden myself. He introduced me to a lot of people, which I wasn't thrilled about, but it was good for me. With his prodding and example, I joined a group and began attending business meetings and taking speaking commitments. Al shared with me his story, past and present. I learned how he became sober and how he stayed sober. Al was a devout Catholic and a great believer in the power of prayer, and he often shared with me the value he found in prayer and his belief in God. But whenever I was in a bind, he didn't just say, "Pray. Ask for God's help." He made other, very practical suggestions that came from his experience.

Once, when I expressed confusion about the meaning of spirituality and all this "God business," especially since I had no belief that God could help,

Al said, "Look Eddie, there's a place in AA for everyone. AA is a very practical program. We come in here after a lifetime of learning bad habits—number one being drinking. We stay sober and go to meetings and try to listen and we begin to understand what those bad habits are. With the help of the program and the people, we get the strength to get rid of some of those bad habits. Then in time we begin to replace them with good habits. Our life gets better and we pass on what we've learned to someone else." I can't express how much that meant to me. It gave me a faith that there was a solution; that things could get better if I kept coming.

I learned to share my feelings with Al. I was always depressed, angry, sad, lonely, you name it. One day when I was down in the mouth again and thinking that this AA meeting stuff was going nowhere, I told Al how helpless I felt. He said, "Eddie, nobody ever died from a feeling. People die from what they do, not from what they feel. You're doing the right things. You're going to meetings, you're sharing with other people, you're helping them and yourself. You'll feel a lot of things as you get sober, but if you keep doing what you're doing you'll be okay."

As time passed I was going to a lot of meetings, but the thought began to creep into my head that maybe I wasn't really an alcoholic. Maybe I needed to go out and get some more drinking in. I even began to think that people were talking about me and saying things like, "Eddie has a lot of problems, but he's not an alcoholic." My story, I thought, wasn't as grand and dramatic as those of the people I'd heard at open meetings. I was afraid to share this with Al, but finally after many weeks when I was nearly convinced that I didn't belong in AA, I told Al what I was thinking. He didn't say, "Pray for acceptance" or "Shut up and sit down, you're an alcoholic." "Eddie," he said, "the only requirement for AA membership is a desire to stop drinking." I'd forgotten that and I thought to myself, So what if they think I'm not an alcoholic? I have that desire. I don't want to drink. I have a right to be here.

Then Al said, "Eddie, do you remember what it was like when you were drinking? The stuff that happened?"

I thought about the blackouts, the accidents, the terror, the shakes, the self-loathing, the nausea, the depletion of energy, the crushing isolation, the unending fear. "Yes," I said.

"Do you want to go back to that?" Al asked.

"No," I responded like a little boy being threatened with banishment to a chair in the corner.

Al said, "Well, you don't have to. You don't ever have to drink again if you don't want to."

I felt liberated after hearing those words. Many people had said to me, "You have to stop drinking." No one had ever said, "You don't have to drink."

Al made AA accessible to a person as sick as I was by showing me how practical it is. I needed to see how it could work for me. He harped on the simplicity of AA, on the wisdom contained in applying ideas like HALT to our lives: try not to get too hungry, angry, lonely, or tired. I abused myself in all of those areas, and still can if I don't stay conscious of that slogan.

First things first. Think. Easy does it. He wove all these phrases into his speech and explained how he applied them in his life and showed me how I could too. Al made me believe that AA is a very practical program that holds the solution to my problem. I'm no longer a doubting Thomas. I've seen AA work in my life.

*Eddie M.*
*Brooklyn, New York*
*July 1997*

# —Just Call Me—

When I first got sober in 1985, because I couldn't stand myself anymore, I was not big on the idea of calling strangers with my problems. But I knew that I was a wreck, that those people at the meetings were not wrecks, and that I wanted to be a former wreck and get what they had. And lo and behold, when I called them, suddenly they weren't strangers anymore.

The women I sponsor nowadays have said sometimes they are reluctant to phone, concerned they will "bother" me or interrupt something I might be doing. If they were just phoning me to tell me about their favorite television show, yes, I might be bothered. But to phone me about Step Four, or the bottle their husband left in the cabinet, or the dream they had last night about the bottomless martini, or to talk about how they're feeling today and what's happening in their lives—that call might just save their lives. And it would help me to remember when my sobriety was new, and I was pretty fuzzy on this whole "life" business, a fuzziness I don't wish to repeat. It also would remind me of why I love to be sober and on my road to recovery. So I listen and learn and remember; you talk and listen and feel better. What a deal!

Looking back over my days of sobriety, I realize I've never had a recov-

---

### "One Little Secret of a Happy Life"—November 1946

One secret of a sweet and happy life is learning to live by the day. It is the long stretches that tire us. We think of life as a whole, running on for us. We cannot carry this load until we are three score and ten. We cannot fight this battle continually for half a century. But really there are no long stretches. Life does not come to us all at one time; it comes only a day at a time. Even tomorrow is never ours until it becomes today, and we have nothing whatever to do with it but to pass down to it a fair and good inheritance in today's work well done, and today's life well lived.

It is a blessed secret this, of living by the day. Anyone can carry his burden, however heavy, till nightfall. Anyone can do his work, however hard, for one day. Anyone can live sweetly, patiently, lovingly, purely, until the sun goes down. And this is all life ever means to us—just one little day. "Do today's duty; fight today's temptations, and do not weaken or distract yourself by looking forward to things you cannot see, and could not understand if you saw them." God gives us nights to shut down upon our little days. We cannot see beyond. Short horizons make life easier and give us one of the blessed secrets of brave, true living.

—*Reflections*, Rev. F. E. Lasance

ering alcoholic not return a phone call or tell me I was pestering her. I've never had a conversation with another AA member I couldn't learn something from, when I really listened. I've never wished I hadn't called or been called—and that includes those very early morning or very late night conversations. I do remember relief when another alcoholic picked up the phone and I could tell her I was thinking about a drink and needed help. I remember a lot of TLC, a lot of good suggestions, a lot of sharing of experience, strength, and hope—a lot of hope, which began growing in my own life—and a lot of laughter.

There are still days when I am in pain, when that pain could be lessened or removed by picking up—the phone, that is. When I call my sponsor, my friends, someone on my home group's phone list, or someone who scribbled their number on a napkin after a meeting, I make progress. My sponsees and I are still learning this one. We don't have to think of a good reason to call; we don't have to plan a speech, select a topic, or rehearse witticisms. If we just call, we help one another stay sober, one call at a time, one connection at a time, one day at a time.

*Judith H.*
*Morristown, New Jersey*
*May 2003*

# —Getting Out Of A Hole—

The first time I drank I was sixteen years old. I blacked out and woke up the next morning lying face down in puke. Just a natural, I guess. I soon figured out how to get drunk and black out without waking up in puke (most of the time). I considered this controlled drinking. I thought blackouts were normal; hell, they were normal for me.

Just after my twentieth birthday I landed in a treatment center after overdosing on alcohol and downers. We had to go to three meetings a week. I remember dreading my turn to say, "I'm Mike and I'm an alcoholic." I didn't believe it.

I now believe, based on experience and observation, that normal drinkers don't spend much time wondering whether or not they're alcoholic, and they rarely end up in treatment centers or attending AA meetings.

As I looked out over the rest of my life from the treatment center, I knew there was no way I could stay sober too long. How could I go to a [Kansas City] Royals game, mow the lawn, or attend a wedding without drinking? I was not faced with these situations at the time, but the suspense was killing me, so I walked over to the convenience store and bought a quart of beer. I remember lying in the weeds behind the treatment center, enjoying my quart and thinking I didn't have a problem with alcohol, I had a problem with treatment centers.

I learned a lot in treatment, played a lot of volleyball, and met some nice people, but didn't put together more than two weeks clean and sober, which wasn't the treatment center's fault. I believed my problem was hard drugs and was partially right. If I could cut out the speed, downers, and hallucinogens, I thought, maybe I could drink normally.

It seemed like a good plan at the time. In fact, it was an improvement. I wasn't as bad as "the people in those meetings." Nine years later, I was that bad.

"Drinking used to be fun, but it's not anymore, and that's too bad," I once heard a newcomer say. That was me. I had a decision to make. I could accept spiritual help or go on to the bitter end. It was a tough choice. I contemplated speeding up the bitter end with a sawed-off shotgun. I sawed off the barrel because I thought it would be undignified to pull the trigger with my toe. I decided to seek help first. I could always blow my brains out if that didn't work.

I took my last drink one week into my second treatment. I was overcome by the obsession to drink after a hot day of fishing. The only thing I could find was a bottle of liqueur with about an ounce left in it. I guess I needed that last drink to show just how powerless over alcohol I was. In my heart, I surrendered. I couldn't drink, and I couldn't not drink. I hoped there was a Higher Power that could restore me to sanity, because I sure couldn't.

I realized that the odds of my staying sober for the rest of my life were not good.

The first step in getting out of a hole is to stop digging. Early sobriety was hell. Not a day went by that the obsession to drink didn't rear its ugly head. Whether it was a song on the radio or a fight with my wife, something always triggered it.

"I'm not going to drink today," I told myself, "but I might tomorrow." On bad days, I said I would get drunk tomorrow, but not today. One particularly rough night I was ready to go to the liquor store. I told myself that I could drink if I went to a meeting first. Something happened during that meeting and I did not take that drink.

I've been sober just over thirteen years and I still believe I could drink tomorrow. I'm an alcoholic. However, it's never tomorrow, it's always today. As long as I don't drink today, tomorrow takes care of itself. One day at a time is the only way I know to stay sober, and it works pretty well.

*Mike N.*
*Topeka, Kansas*
*February 2006*

# —Gladitude!—

For years I felt a little out of step at meetings when the subject was gratitude. I didn't feel grateful—therefore I must not be grateful. This began to change recently when a friend suggested I make a gratitude list of little things—like having warm blankets and a roof that doesn't leak. I found that making these lists after getting into bed at night helped me wind down and go to sleep. It felt good. It surely was nice that the bed was warm and the roof didn't leak. If I woke during the night, this same practice and the good feelings it brought would help me fall back to sleep.

But what about the big things? I still didn't feel grateful. Not in proportion to what God had given me. My lack of true gratitude not only made me feel awkward at meetings, but also awkward with God.

A little progress called out for more. I went to my sponsor and shared the wonderful tip my friend had given me. It was making me feel good. But I still felt a little guilty for not responding properly to God's blessings. He said, "Is there anything you are glad about?" "Well, sure," I told him. "There is lots of stuff I'm glad about, but I'm not grateful. Or not grateful enough."

"Well, if you are glad about something," he said, "then put it on your list and stick with that for awhile. Worry about gratitude later."

Well, that's just what I'm doing. And it works! I'm glad about so much. I am so blessed by all God has made possible in my life. After sharing these insights at a meeting recently, and how glad I was to have them, my friend Ron nodded, then said, "Yes ... gladitude!"

I like it, Ron. Gladitude! And I'm going to use it.

*Bob H.*
*Long Beach, California*
*December 1993*

# Experience, Strength, and Hope

*Alcoholics Anonymous is a fellowship of men and women who share their experience, strength and hope with each other that they may solve their common problem and help others to recover from alcoholism.*

—AA Preamble

Alcoholics Anonymous is not a theoretical program. It's one based on what works to keep alcoholics like us sober. Our Big Book, for example, represents the hard-earned experience of the first one hundred members of our Fellowship. Our meetings offer more sharing of experience, as do sponsorship and friendship. When anyone has questions about the AA program, when support and advice is sought, we don't offer theories but try to answer from our own experience. Perhaps that's the greatest gift we have to share—to say, "This is what I did. It worked for me. Maybe it will work for you." We get strength and hope from hearing others talk about how they stayed away from a drink—and also found moments of joy and freedom.

The stories in this section form a kind of beginner's meeting discussion. You'll find useful suggestions, insights, and solutions to common problems—and plenty of strength and hope.

# —Insanity B—

A lot of people have trouble with the sanity clause in the Second Step. "How can a higher power restore me to sanity when I was never insane?" they protest.

Not me. As I often tell my home group: When the attendants let me out of the fourth-floor ward at the hospital, they gave me a little certificate attesting to my insanity.

But even if the protesters don't have certificates like mine, some old-timer can usually persuade them that they need to be restored to sanity. Usually it just takes the old standby: "We demonstrated our insanity by doing the same thing over and over again expecting a different result."

I sure did that.

Now I have come to believe that my drinking insanity is only one form of the craziness to which we AAs are prone. I call it Insanity A. Insanity B is finding out what works for you—and then not doing it.

I'm not one of those wise AAs who decided one day to surrender. I came crawling into my first meeting because I was whipped, beaten. My marriage was going under. I had been fired from a job for the second time. I had barely recovered from a suicide attempt and had just been released after ten days in a psych ward.

For the first few weeks, I sat through meetings, comprehending little. After a while I dimly gathered that I was supposed to get something called "a sponsor." I asked John G. because he was an older man and might help me save my marriage. And he was an industrialist and might help me get a job.

In our first meeting, John G. talked tough. "Forget about saving your marriage," he said. "Forget about getting a job. Just don't drink, go to meetings, say your prayers, and be grateful."

I saw immediately that he didn't understand my problems so I patiently explained them more clearly. He interrupted me with, "Forget all that. Just don't drink, go to meetings, say your prayers, and be grateful."

"You," I blurted, "are the meanest (bleep) I ever met."

John G. did not become my sponsor.

But his words never left me. I picked up my attendance at meetings, chose a sponsor for no other reason than I thought he had something I wanted, and worked the Steps.

I also remembered something else John G. said to me. "It's all right to make a gratitude list," he said, "but never forget that the things on that list can go away. And when that happens, be grateful anyway."

My marriage of thirty-eight years did break up, by the way. And even in sobriety, I got fired from another job. I've had some more ups and downs. But the Promises have pretty much come true for me.

It's been years since those first AA meetings. I haven't had another drink. I've resumed the career of my youth as a news reporter. I'm now an international broadcaster living overseas with my new wife in one of the most beautiful cities of this world. The Promises after the Ninth Step in the Big Book have—it's worth repeating—pretty much come true for me.

Most of the time I have a long gratitude list, but even when it runs short, I'm grateful. So why do I have these periods when my serenity is disturbed, when I long to be a big shot on the job or when I get inexplicably irritable with my wife?

I was visiting my old haunts in Washington, D.C. on a trip a few years ago, and I went to a downtown meeting. I heard someone say, "I used to pray and meditate every day and work my program. And I felt great. But now I find I'm not doing those things so much. And I feel awful. What should I do?"

I laughed inwardly, and I was still chuckling as I walked down the street after the meeting. But then I suddenly realized—that man was speaking for me.

Fairly often, I forget John G.'s admonition, "Just don't drink, go to meetings, say your prayers, and be grateful." I stop doing those things. I become grasping, worrying about things that hardly matter, critical of my family and friends. And it's my serenity that fades.

I know what works for me, but sometimes I don't do it. Insanity B.

*Don H.*
*Prague, Czechoslovakia*
*February 2005*

# —The Secret—

I hung around the AA program for eight years before I finally surrendered to a Higher Power and AA. Each time I walked through the doors (usually drunk), I was greeted with open arms, and throughout each meeting I understood that "these people" had found something I wanted: The Secret to staying sober.

After each meeting, I used to corner whomever had the most sobriety and ask them what The Secret was, and each time I was told that to find out I had to keep coming to meetings.

This was not an acceptable answer! I didn't have time to go to meetings when I had so many important things to do: I had a wife, a house, a family, a job, etc.

So I did it my way. After only seven treatment centers, a mental institution, a divorce, and my local hospitals telling me that I was no longer welcome, did it begin to dawn on me that my way might be flawed.

And I still didn't know The Secret. I finally convinced (begged) one of the treatment centers I had been in to give me one more chance, promising that I would do anything to get sober. They accepted me only on the condition that I commit myself to a long-term treatment facility one hundred miles away, and as soon as an opening became available, off I went.

A year later (six months more than required), I moved to a small town in southern Illinois and started college because I knew I couldn't stay sober in the retail business I had been in.

Today, I'm married to a wonderful woman who is also in the program and am continuing my education beginning with my understanding of how it works. The Secret is, there is no Secret! Working the Steps with a sponsor, going to meetings, helping others, and above all, keeping God and sobriety first have kept me sober almost five years now. I always had heard that things in plain sight are the hardest to find!

*Scott J.*
*Vandalia, Illinois*
*February 2001*

# —Stick With The Stickers—

For those of us who hit bottom and asked for help in my military setting, part of the protocol was to attend a two-week alcohol and drug addiction class while being introduced to Alcoholics Anonymous meetings. On my first day in this class, the seasoned, recovering alcoholic up front declared that we would be able to obtain sobriety if we did just five things. As he reached for the chalk to write on the board, I reached for my pen and paper. I desperately wanted to stay sober and was eager to learn the "secrets" I had not been able to find on my own. He wrote:

1. Don't drink. (When everyone sighed, he added that the remaining four ensured #1.)
2. Go to meetings.
3. Get a sponsor.
4. Read the Big Book.
5. Stick with the stickers.

The rest of the day the class focused on the disease of alcoholism and, while I was interested and listening, I kept pondering the five things I needed to do to achieve lasting sobriety.

I had no previous exposure to recovery, and I had some incorrect assumptions about it. I thought that meetings were classes to teach us where we had gone wrong with our sober attempts, and after completing them, we would go on with our lives. I thought the slogans on the wall posters, coffee mugs, and bumper stickers were summary reminders that would help us stay true to the lessons learned in the classes. So, I made every effort to read and memorize all the slogans on all the bumper stickers that I could find. I craved sobriety, and was determined to "Stick with the stickers."

So, for the first two weeks, my program consisted of not drinking, listening at meetings, planning to get a sponsor when I found the perfect one, reading the Big Book, and sticking with bumper stickers. When I heard people in meetings say that they had been sober for longer than a month or two, I felt sorry for them for being such slow learners. I had been a secret drinker and learning to share in recovery was a very slow process. I kept to myself and rarely talked to anyone at meetings, so I never asked why people who had been sober for a while were still at meetings.

On the last day of class, our instructor again listed the five secrets on the board, only this time he commented on number five: "When you're at meetings, look around and find those folks who keep coming back," he said. "Stick with those stickers. They are the winners, as recovery is not only about not drinking but also about learning to live happy, joyous, and free lives while sober."

I nearly fell out of my chair with this news. This was a life-long program? I needed to do more than follow a few slogans on bumper stickers? I had to

---

**From "Small but Mighty"—March 2006**

In the meetings I attend, newcomers sometimes ask me how I've been able to stay sober so long. My answer is always the same: every morning, the first thing I do is say three magic words—God, help me.

—Jack H., Kissimmee, Florida

become part of this "fellowship" that I heard about at meetings? I should get close to these people? My head spun, and my heart raced with panic. Only by the grace of God was I willing to listen and try to follow his suggestions.

Today, I am sixteen years sober and living an incredibly happy, joyous, and free life. I wouldn't trade it for anything, and I owe it all to Alcoholics Anonymous. The program and the Fellowship have not only enabled me to live without alcohol but enriched my life beyond my wildest dreams. The Fellowship holds the closest friends I have ever known, and I trust my life to them on a daily basis. Whenever I hear the slogan, "Stick with the stickers," I smile and say a prayer of gratitude for both the sticker-slogans of my original interpretation and the recovering folks who have gone before me and so graciously passed the program on.

*Nancy S.*
*Renton, Washington*
*August 2006*

# —A Lady After All—

From the age of five, I always felt different from everyone else. I was taller than everybody else, felt uglier than everybody else, and as an only child, I knew I was lonelier than everybody else. I could never measure up to my expectations and I didn't think I measured up to anyone else's either.

My first drink was at age thirteen. I drank homemade dandelion wine with my alcoholic great-aunt. Suddenly, I was Ginger Rogers, Marilyn Monroe, and Eve Arden all rolled into one. I had arrived.

I didn't drink again until my wedding day, five years later. I remember very little about that day. After that, I found that if I drank I could fit in with a crowd; I could be part of a group instead of a loner. I drank to have sex. I drank with my husband and at my husband. I drank in joy, in sadness, in anger. I just drank.

Next came the first divorce, and I was the original party girl from then on. I found myself crawling in and out of different barroom bathroom windows, running away from my actions. I'd sit on a barstool in my ratty mink stole, the hem of my skirt tucked into my girdle, thinking I was "hip, slick, and cool." I was a lady, after all. I drank wearing a mink stole so I had to be a lady. I ended up in strange places with strange men and thought I was having the time of my life. Often, I had to call someone the next day to see if I had indeed had a good time!

After that, I went on the wagon for several years. I was living in the Canadian bush, fifty miles from the nearest town and neighbor. It was too far to go for a drink, especially in the winter and twenty feet of snow. Finally I moved to a small town in British Columbia and met a lady who offered to teach me to knit at the pub every afternoon. Of course, I had to be sociable and hoist a pint or two. I controlled my drinking until I could get home to "Harvey,"— Harvey's Bristol Cream Sherry, that is. I thought I was in hog heaven since I was drinking like a lady: everybody knows that ladies drink sherry.

Eight years later, I returned to the United States, and my drinking career continued. I'd go to work with a big brown aspirin bottle full of Canadian Club whiskey in my purse for emergencies. After work, I'd stop for a quick one and invariably my son would have to call, hours later, begging me to come home. This continued through another marriage.

---

**From "Bad Habits"—November 2007**

AA gave me good habits to replace my bad habits. Instead of sitting in self-pity, I was told to hit meetings early and do service by helping to set up chairs and doing whatever was needed (usefulness). Instead of fighting, I was told to do something nice for people without getting caught (humility). Instead of sitting in my head, I was told to go down my home group's phone list, call other members on their sobriety birthdays, and wish them a wonderful day (thinking of others). Instead of taking friends hostage, I was told to meet at least two new females wherever I went and reach out the hand of AA to them (giving back what was given to me).

—Tina H., Waukesha, Wisconsin

Then, we moved to Southern California, and I immediately hated the Mojave Desert and all of California. I realized I'd lose my paycheck (my hubby) if I didn't slow down on the booze. I discovered prescription drugs could help me, although alcohol was my drug of choice. Hubby would take care of me if I was "sick" but not if I was a drunk. I ended up with a fifth-a-day habit, and a $600-a-month pharmacy bill. I was going to three doctors and two hospitals. The blackouts were beginning again but I was just "sick." I didn't have a drinking problem—not me. I was having trouble on the job, in my marriage, with my family, with other men, with finances—with everything except the law. That was because I was married to a law-enforcement officer. I once ended up in an airline terminal in Minneapolis, Minnesota, dressed in the same ratty mink stole, talking about going ice fishing. I came home and tried to straighten up.

I went back to church, read every self-help book I could find, but that didn't last long. Soon I was back in the bars, trying to work, keep Hubby from knowing what I was doing, and yet party heavily.

My next major blackout found me in Jeddi, Saudi Arabia. I'm told that I dared some airline pilots to smuggle me into Saudi Arabia to see just how red the Red Sea was. It isn't red, but a beautiful blue, away from shore. It took a week to smuggle me out of the country and back to Los Angeles.

Then I knew I needed help, but I had to go to one more party. Again, I experienced another blackout. I was told on my nineteenth AA anniversary that I had been evicted from the San Bernardino chapter of the Hell's Angels for being too crazy. The man who evicted me was celebrating thirteen years of continuous sobriety that evening.

I was getting sicker—physically and emotionally. Spiritually, I was dead. I had reached the point where I couldn't live but I couldn't die. My only son, the apple of my eye, finally confronted me with an ultimatum. "Mother, either you get help now, or I will leave and you will never hear or see me again as long as you live," he told me. Somehow I knew he meant it. I called the crisis hot line and was in the hospital a few hours later. My fear of losing my son was great enough that I would ask for help from anyone. It took thirty days to detox from the alcohol and drugs before I walked into my first meeting of Alcoholics Anonymous.

I entered that meeting weighing 320 pounds, standing six feet tall, wearing tight blue jeans, a western shirt, cowboy boots, a Stetson hat, and a .45 pistol on my hip. Slapping the gun on the table, I said, "All right, you turkeys, I want what you have, this thing you call sobriety." A small man with a big bushy mustache slid the gun away from me and growled, "Sit down and shut up. I'll tell you when, where, and if you can talk." I promptly did what he said, and it was the first direction I had taken in a long time.

The group told me: "Keep coming back. Don't drink between meetings. Bring the body, the mind will follow. Put the plug in the jug. Take the cotton out of one ear, put that cotton in your mouth. Leave the cotton in one ear only so what you hear won't whistle through that empty cavity. Be willing to put as much energy into your sobriety as you put into your drinking. You have a dis-

---

**From "What Do I Like Best?"—March 2003**

My first AA meeting was in South Florida, in a retirement community where my mother lives. I never imagined that I'd find any common ground with all those elderly, white Americans, but I was in for another surprise—it was a women's meeting! I didn't stay the duration, but was instantly struck by its simplicity and by the lack of any judgment that the ladies exuded, and I looked forward to my next meeting, which had men in it. I went. Again the welcome was real. Neither my youth, my race, my newness, nor my foreignness concerned them. All they appeared to see was that I finally admitted my powerlessness over alcohol. That was enough for them, and I came to believe they had what I needed. I had a social experience with spiritual repercussions: the same night, I earnestly asked the Higher Power to heal what I could not, and have not had a serious urge since. In Trinidad, I found something similar: a kaleidoscope of people with one common problem, and one common interest. I could relate in a real and profound way.

—Joseph C., Port of Spain

ease called alcoholism. If you were a diabetic, you probably would be taking insulin. The medicine for alcoholism is AA and you need to take a dose daily.""I was told to take it one day at a time—"But if a day is too long, cut it down." I was told to attend thirty meetings in thirty days. At the end of thirty days, I was told, "Since you are such a sick puppy, you need to 're-up' for another thirty days." They kept harping on "Keep Coming Back." It had been years since I had been asked to return anywhere. My thought was, "I'll fix them, I will go back."

Members told me I needed to be willing to go to any length for my sobriety. That meant, if necessary, giving up husbands, children, jobs, houses, cars, friends, etc., to stay sober. I was to get a sponsor, a person who walked her talk, one I respected. I didn't have to like her; liking would come later.

I was now in school, a school to learn how to live life without booze. The Big Book of Alcoholics Anonymous was my textbook, and I was to read the first 164 pages only. I was not to memorize it. "Always have to search for what you want to find, that way you will learn more each time you pick up the book, no matter how long you are in the Fellowship," I was told. "This way you will learn to live the Twelve Steps and Twelve Traditions and not become an AA guru."

I also was told to be at a meeting fifteen minutes early and stay fifteen minutes late. I was to ask questions, listen, and socialize with those who had more continuous sobriety. I was to strive for quality sobriety, for often quality would bring quantity. I was to work the Twelve Steps and Twelve Traditions to the best of my ability. Honesty comes with practice, they said, and this thing called sobriety comes with practice, too.

People suggested that I needed a Higher Power or my sobriety might not last. I'd been a church member for years, but I didn't have a personal relationship with my Higher Power, whom I chose to call God, until then.

I was also told, "Your first year is a gift." In my first year, my stepfather died, and I was bitten by a rattlesnake and a black widow spider. I had a heart attack and a stroke. My three step-children were killed by a drunk driver. I went to meetings, did not drink, and used the Fellowship of AA to get me through that first year. If the first year was a gift—thank you, but no more gifts. I will work for my sobriety and will continue to do so as long as I live.

Today, I can face death (mine as well as that of others), remarriages, and illness. I'm able to accept responsibility for others and myself. I can face poverty as well as affluence. I'm employable, adaptable, and teachable—thanks to the program of Alcoholics Anonymous and God. I'm learning to live life on life's terms and to enjoy it. To accept the good and the bad, and to be grateful for both. I have a long way to go, and I pray I never give up growing spiritually, emotionally, and mentally.

This program will work for you too, if you keep coming back. Don't drink or use between meetings. Be willing to be willing to follow directions and you will find your life changing in all areas. Today, I don't have the home, the husband, the three cars in the garage. I have one old clunker that takes me to meetings. I am not financially well off, but I have a peace of mind I never dreamed possible. My needs are always met—and even some of my wishes. I am truly happy for the first time in my life. Thank you, AA. Today I am a real lady.

*Sharon F.*
*Milwaukie, Oregon*
*June 1999*

# —Paradoxes of Sobriety—

September 17, 1997 marked my thirty-second year in this great Fellowship of Alcoholics Anonymous. In all those years, if I've had any bad days, I can't remember them. AA has taught me that I'm the architect of my own success or happiness. The quality of my sobriety is up to me—it will be what I want it to be. The truth is that my alcoholism is the best thing that ever happened to me, because it brought me to AA and this wonderful new way of life.

Over the years, I've made some observations about the AA program which can be summed up by the phrase "the paradoxes of sobriety." The dictionary defines paradox as a statement that's true but appears to be false or self-contradictory. What follows are a few examples.

You have to surrender to win. The keys are giving up the futile struggle, admitting we're powerless over alcohol, and turning our lives and will over to the care of God as we understand him. The only way we can beat a Heavyweight Champion of the World is not to get into the ring with him. But we need help to stay out of the ring. We can't do it alone.

It's not the end, it's the beginning. Newcomers to AA are preoccupied with the thought of never drinking again. They are guilty of "forever" thinking, and coming into AA seems like the end. In reality, it's the beginning of a new life. The "weller than well" theory tells us that we can enjoy a better life for having—and solving—our drinking problem.

It's not forever, it's just for today. The great secret of AA is living a day at a time. That's all we have anyway. Living a day at a time doesn't mean we can't set some goals or plan our vacation or retirement, only that we can't live emotionally beyond the twenty-fours allotted to us.

AA is a spiritual program, not a religious one. Getting outside of ourselves—getting rid of the hate, hostility, and resentment—is the spiritual purpose of AA. We are asked to find our own Higher Power, as we understand him, to bring focus to our lives. While we are told to "leave religion at the door" of AA, some of us find a way back to our religion, but as an adjunct to, not to the exclusion of, the spirituality of AA.

The more dependent we are on the AA program, the more independent we become. The more we commit to AA, the more freedom we enjoy. Happiness and peace of mind are the by-products of working the Steps, attending meetings regularly, reading the Big Book, and getting involved in the Fellowship. AA gives us a life that sets us free.

You have to give it away to keep it. We can't hoard the sobriety we enjoy. We need to share our experience, strength, and hope with each other to stay sober. In fact, we are never "even"; we always get more than we give.

What are the rewards of AA? Let's start with life itself and freedom, and go on to self-respect, self-esteem, and straight thinking, new friends, and pride in ourselves and our families. We have a Higher Power we might never have found otherwise. AA gives us a Ph.D. in life and a black belt in common sense. Thanks to AA, we've become "converts to life."

At an open meeting some years ago, the speaker said he was proud to be at the meeting. Proud? I'd never heard that before. He went on to say, "I'm proud to be with the people who saved my life." So am I.

*Joe H.*
*Keego Harbor, Michigan*
*June 1998*

# —Never Sober Today Before—

"I've never been sober today before." This is one of the most profound slogans I've ever heard in AA. I'll never forget that cold winter's night when Joe D. first shared it with me. I was going through a rough time and churning with so much emotion that Joe explained it to me in simple terms.

In my second year sober, things were getting "different" before getting "better." I was going through a painful divorce, losing a home and half my stuff, and, worst, I wasn't living with my young daughter any more.

Joe and I frequently got coffee after the meeting. As he took me back to my car, he said, "You need to think about this: You've never been sober today before."

My mind tried to process what I had heard. He must have sensed my wheels spinning as I looked out over the empty parking lot.

"Well, have you ever been sober on this day before?" he asked.

"No," I said after a long pause.

"You never know what will be required of you on any particular day," he said.

Suddenly, in one of those rare cathartic moments, I got it, in the way you can only "get it" in AA. I had to be spiritually prepared daily for whatever came my way. Pain or joy, I could feel it sober. If I turned to my Higher Power, no matter what, he would provide whatever I needed to face the day sober.

After twenty years, I still use this slogan and include it in my lead. It helps me focus, with gratitude, on the opportunities each day presents. If there are challenges, I remember other days when what seemed impossible was made possible. Although I've never been sober today before, I count on my Higher Power to keep me sober as he has done on all those other days before.

*John Y.*
*Huntington, West Virginia*
*August 2006*

# A Design for Living

*A new life has been given us ...*
*a "design for living" that really works.*
— Alcoholics Anonymous

A few years after AA's birth in 1935, Bill W., Dr. Bob, and other early members worked out a set of suggested guidelines to help the newly sober man or woman. It was clear that bare sobriety wasn't enough— drunks needed a program of recovery, a way to deal with the fear, self-pity, lack of faith, and resentment that led back to drinking. The twelve suggested Steps became that program—and the bedrock of the new Fellowship—helping millions of people stay sober.

To many, the Steps seem daunting at first. But many old-timers, relying on the slogan "Keep It Simple," say they began by reading the Big Book, the "Twelve and Twelve," and going to Step meetings. We hope the stories in this section will provide more lights along the path.

# —Get With the Program—

When I first got to AA, I heard a lot of talk centering around the word "program" — as in, "That's how I work my program." But what the heck was a program, anyway? I knew I needed one, so I decided to ask someone about it. I asked Jane who was setting up chairs and making the coffee for our evening meeting.

"Jane," I asked. "What's your program?"

"I go to fourteen meetings a week, I'm secretary for five of them, I answer phones at the central office three nights a week, I have one sponsor for each of my character defects, plus a Big Book sponsor, and a backup to help me when the others aren't around."

"Incredible!" I said. "How long have you been sober?"

"Ninety-three days, nineteen hours, and twenty-seven minutes," she said. "And I'm doing just great!"

Well, I loved to hear what Jane said at meetings, but I was exhausted just watching her go by. So I did what most of us do when a question is beyond us—I called my sponsor.

"Read the Big Book," he said. "Chapter Five says something about 'program.' See if you can find it."

I somehow failed to see it, but I sure came to love that chapter. Then, one crisp fall day as I was driving to work and listening to one of my AA tapes, I finally heard it: "Here are the Steps we took, which are suggested as a program of recovery." Son of a gun, the Steps are the program!

One of the dictionary definitions of the word "program" is "any organized list of procedures; schedule." And that's exactly what the Steps came to be for me.

First of all, nothing can begin unless I take Step One. I haven't yet figured out what happened the day I finally went to my first meeting—that hadn't happened in the previous twenty years—but I went, and I'm still here. I had to take Step One and quit drinking to start the process of physical, mental, and spiritual recovery.

Step Two was the next logical place to go. I started to understand that while I didn't believe in churches, I had to see that something or someone was working in my life that hadn't been there before. The insanity part wasn't hard to grasp—I had scars on my arms and news clippings in my desk to prove it. Then, as my mind further unclouded, I could accept that my life had gotten on track and that the new "engineer" was doing better than I ever had. Step Three fit into the schedule perfectly.

Step Four follows Three because, with someone like a Higher Power on my side, what could I possibly be afraid of? While doing Four, I wrote about meeting my soon-to-be ex-wife. My mind was thinking that she was attractive and had many personality traits that complemented mine as my pencil wrote, "I was looking for someone to take the place of my mother." I dropped the pencil! Those words hadn't been in my conscious mind. For heaven's sake, I thought. She even looks like my mother. Five foot three, brown hair and eyes, little dusting of freckles. Well, I'll be ....

Step Five is fantastic. Once I had the character defects identified, I wanted to do Five. With all this stuff out in the open, no one could trip me up

---

**From "Happily Whole"—March 2005**

When I came to AA in 1971, I was told that all the answers to my questions could be found in the Big Book, specifically in "The Doctor's Opinion," the appendices, and, more importantly, the first 164 pages. I find that statement to be as true today as it was thirty-three years ago.

I sobered up while on active duty in the U.S. Navy. During my first two years in AA, I moved between five states, three foreign countries, and ten months aboard ship. By working the Steps as they are written in the Big Book and with infrequent meetings and a dependence on God as I understand him, I have, I think, lost the compulsion to drink, and, as the foreword to the "Twelve and Twelve" says, have become "happily and usefully whole."

—Jim S., Virginia Beach, Virginia

with some awful discovery of something in my past. What a feeling of relief. Now Six and Seven became possible and necessary. I very much wanted to get rid of the stuff that didn't work. That's the stuff that hurts! I wanted to become a friend among friends, a worker among workers—a contributing member of the human race.

The first Seven Steps, then, got me okay with me and with this Higher Power character. But I discovered that I still lived in a world of people I had to face every day ... and there were problems in this. Step Eight would identify those problems and get me ready for Nine. Eight was my preparation for speaking to persons I had harmed, which was a really big task for me. These were the folks who I dreaded seeing. And of course it was in seeing them that my greatest healing was realized.

I don't work Step Ten; it works me, especially when I'm screwing something up! My stomach starts to tighten and I can't put it off to the end of a day. I've got to stop right there and take a different tack or I'm going to be absolutely miserable until I do. A visitor to my home group meeting once said that Step Ten allows him "to clean up the wreckage of the present." That's pretty much on the mark in my experience.

Ten has to come before Step Eleven because I can't get quiet to meditate or pray until I've dealt with lingering problems from the day just past.

Prayer and meditation. Talking to God, as you understand God, and then listening for the answers. Amazing! You just kind of know the folks who work this Step by who they are. They have an inner calm about them that tells everyone they're actually connected to a power greater than themselves. I'm getting there, but I've still got quite a way to go.

Now for Step Twelve. My "spiritual awakening" is still underway and will be for the rest of my life. Sometimes I "carry the message" by just being a sober presence in an AA meeting, a presence that says to another alcoholic that there is hope. And the practice of "these principles" is evident in my daily doing of whatever I do in a manner that doesn't harm myself or others.

The single greatest thing I've gotten from following this program is the relationship I have with a Higher Power as I now understand it. At a meeting, I overheard a lady saying that "AA is like a wagon train. Some of us drive wagons and some of us are scouts. And whenever the scouts come back, they tell us it's really bad out there. But if you ask the wagon-master for help, then you can drive a wagon—and you don't have to be a scout." I think she's on to something and I intend to keep coming back until I find out what it is!

*Dennis O.*

*Naples, Italy*

*January 1994*

# —Naming the Negatives?—

The Fourth Step attracted me almost as I arrived at the doors of Alcoholics Anonymous. I came to AA full of guilt and remorse for all the bad things I'd done — for example, being an unfaithful wife, not doing my job to the best of my ability and still expecting the highest rewards, and being unresponsive to other people's needs. I was totally self-centered, while at the same time I was thought of by others as being a good wife to a man who drank too much and ran around, being loyal to a job for twelve years, and being so sweet (I never expressed an opinion!). But the way I was viewed by others was not the way I felt inside.

I heard AAs talking about getting rid of the guilt of the past by taking the Fourth and Fifth Steps. I wanted to get rid of my feelings of fear, frustration, and depression, and I became willing to go to any length to accomplish that.

The first thing to do was to make a decision that since I couldn't handle my own life (look at the mess it was in), I could find my own Higher Power to which I could turn over my life and my will. After that, I'd be able to look at myself and take responsibility for my past actions.

I certainly didn't know how to put names to my feelings because for years I'd practiced not giving information to others about how I felt and what I thought. If I had problems, I was to solve them myself; hadn't I been taught to be self-sufficient? As I went to meetings and heard others talk about their feelings, I came to recognize some of mine. I came to understand that my natural instincts "for the sex relation, for material and emotional security, and for companionship" need not run my life in a negative way.

Early on, one of my ways of staying sober had been to write down my feelings and questions and new things I learned. At the beginning of my sobriety I would ride home from a meeting on a bus. My small notebook in my purse was there to write down any thoughts I'd had during the meeting I'd just left.

After about fifteen months (and a couple of journals), I went to someone with a good solid sobriety and asked for help in turning my notes into a Fourth Step. He suggested that we meet and I arrived, notebooks in hand. He started me talking, leading me in a discussion of my problems in the areas of sex, society, and security (as suggested by the Big Book). He suggested that I look at pride, greed, lust, anger, gluttony, envy, and sloth. We talked for about three hours and covered every area of my life I had problems in. I found I could put names to my negative feelings and see their source.

What a relief to tell someone about myself without any threat of retaliation or condemnation. I realized I wasn't the worst, most immoral woman alive. I was no different from others who shared at meetings, neither worse nor better, and I wasn't strange or different. When I looked at my assets, I realized that I hadn't set out to harm others or intentionally behaved in an unacceptable manner. I wasn't a bad person; I was a sick person trying to get better. I was a worthwhile human being.

People talk about having a spiritual experience after taking the Fourth Step. What happened to me was that I learned about the person I had been. I looked at my "emotional deformities" so I could "move toward their correction." I now had a better sense of direction concerning what areas I needed to work on. As *Twelve Steps and Twelve Traditions* explains, "... a brand-new kind of confidence is born, and the sense of relief at finally facing ourselves is indescribable."

Since that first inventory, I've taken many Fourth Steps. When my marriage was in trouble, I looked at my part in the problem, at where I'd been wrong. I had no fear in looking at my behavior because I'd been trying in sobriety to be a good wife and companion. I found that my dependence on someone I considered stronger was misdirected. I was frightened of life and hadn't grown up; I felt dominated but in some areas I myself was the one who dominated. I put demands on another person which couldn't possibly be met. I tried to manipulate my husband to meet what I thought were my needs, when I really didn't know my needs.

A few years later, when my marriage had broken up and I'd met someone in whom I was interested, I took an inventory of my relationships with the other men who'd been in my life (father, brothers, friends, lovers), whether causing trouble or not. I didn't want to get into a relationship where I made the same mistakes over again. In this inventory, I found the same dependencies growing out of fear, self-pity, worry, greed, possessiveness, anger, and a lack of confidence in myself.

Today, when a particular problem can't be covered by a daily Tenth Step, I find it natural to use the Fourth Step. I start with the First Step and see where I'm powerless, I recognize that a Higher Power can help me, and I use the Third Step prayer as a preliminary move toward the Fourth Step. After taking a Fifth Step, I use the subsequent Steps to help me handle the problem.

The Fourth Step lets me look at myself, look into my fear of not getting something I want or of losing something I have, get a perspective on my character defects, and move forward to try to establish true partnerships with other human beings: all in order to be "one in a family, to be a friend among friends, to be a worker among workers, to be a useful member of society."

*Sherry G.*
*Riverdale, Michigan*
*April 1997*

# —A Lifetime Supply—

Coming into AA and finding the acceptance and love I'd sought in a bottle was a relief beyond description, but reading the Steps was a shock. Fortunately for me, my home group did not hammer the Steps into newcomers. Rather, they talked a lot about the Slogans and the need to not drink a day at a time. I needed that.

During a discussion of Step Seven, I made the statement, "If my shortcomings and character defects are removed, there will be nothing left!" I need not have feared. What I've learned since then is that I have more than a lifetime's supply of character defects. My Higher Power and I can't get rid of them all in my allotted time on this earth.

More importantly, I've learned that if I simply let go of a character defect—release it—my Higher Power will replace it with a character asset. As I release anger, I find that I am friendlier. As I release hate, I become more loving. As I release fear, I become more secure. I don't have to go out looking for friendliness, love, security, or any other trait that I desire. I just have to give up the feelings that are manifestations of my character defects and the good automatically flows into my life. And I used to think that I would become hollow without my character defects!

So, how does it work? Daily. On a daily basis I choose not to drink—or to fear, hate, be angry, or indulge in any other defect that's raising its ugly head. They're all there waiting, and when given a chance they charge into the center of my life and try to take over. But when I work Step Seven, I find that my life is filled with good, and people actually like to be around me—something they never did in my drinking days.

C.
*Kathmandu, Nepal*
*July 1995*

# —How an Atheist Works the Steps—

My life was in shambles, and I was desperate. Following a third botched suicide attempt, I was threatened with commitment to a mental hospital. Or I could call AA. I chose AA. But I was skeptical that it was the answer because I thought I was just crazy. I thought using alcohol and drugs was a result of my problems, not a cause. I also knew that AA's program relies on a belief system that I didn't have. I told the woman who picked me up for my first meeting of my concerns. She assured me that there would be a place in AA for a crazed heathen like me.

Encouraged by the sense of relief and the lessening of fear that I felt at that first meeting, I decided right then not to struggle over God stuff. I figured if there is a God, I'd lose the battle; if there is none, it would be pointless, wasted effort. That was just under thirty-two years ago, and I have been sober and an active member of AA ever since. That means I have always gone to meetings (mainstream ones—no special meetings for atheist/agnostic members), I have relied on many close and trusted friends in the Fellowship, I do group service, and I try to carry the message to other alcoholics.

Despite my lack of God-understanding, which continues to this day, the Fellowship of AA has been an effective way for me to stay sober. Sober AA members have the experience of recovery, and they listen sympathetically and critically, providing advice and guidance. Their example helps me learn how to live without having to drink—ever, if I don't want to. I have found through my own experiences and observation of others that it doesn't matter what I believe; it's what I do that counts. AA provides the basis for learning what to do.

At the first meeting, I was told the obvious: not drinking is an absolute requirement for sobriety. I didn't drink, and I did whatever was necessary to avoid drinking. That required going to many meetings and reading AA books and other self-help guides. It meant accepting that people would talk about God. It meant breaking off some ill-advised associations and developing a circle of friends I could call on when I felt shaky. It meant getting involved as secretary or other group servant. It meant being willing to lie awake, or be fearful, or feel anxious, or be lonely at times. Life wasn't always easy: I suffered from depression for a time and had to concentrate on "One Day at a Time." Nevertheless, I lost my desire to drink and actually felt good about abstaining.

After I dried out and could begin to understand my condition, I wanted wellness. I wanted to live as a better person in harmony with others and with my circumstances, to be free of the chaos and conflict that had riddled my drinking life. I was told I probably needed to change every aspect of how I acted and reacted and that the AA Steps and program could help me. But what about those God Steps?

Someone once pointed out that the Steps could be considered either a description of changes that occur in recovery or a road map for making those changes. So I decided not to worry about whether I was taking the right route; instead, I focused on changing my behavior. I didn't try to force my beliefs to fit someone else's Step Three or concentrate on doing Steps Four and Five the "Twelve and Twelve" way. I simply listened to what others said about handling life events and tried what they had done in various situations. I haven't thought of my efforts as "doing the Steps," and yet I see that what I try to do approximates the direction of recovery described in the fifth chapter of *Alcoholics Anonymous*.

Besides not drinking, the most important habit I have tried to develop is not fighting circumstances. I try to accept reality instead of trying to control it. When I make that adjustment, the struggle ends and I find the freedom of knowing there is nothing more I can or must do. That sense of freedom came first when I recognized and accepted my powerlessness over alcohol (Step One). It is available in all life's adventures, if I fit myself to the flow of life (Step Three).

I remind myself regularly to trust the inner resource of the well person inside and the outer resource of the group. The track record of others and my own history show me that I can get through whatever comes, if I am patient and do what makes sense on a daily basis. This fills the intent of Step Two for me and also provides the benefits of Step Three.

I take responsibility for my actions and feelings. I think this is what Steps Four and Ten are all about—knowing and admitting my part in all my interactions and not making excuses for myself.

Consulting with others before acting on important issues and discussing past actions that bring me discomfort are integral to my life now. I am not experienced enough or objective enough to evaluate past, present, or future without a sounding board. This habit keeps my life running more smoothly and is pretty close to what Step Five describes.

I have made a great effort to stop doing those things that make me feel guilty or that diminish my opinion of myself. The burden of guilt—or fear of being found out—might lead me to seek solace in drinking. I try to do no harm and let others live their own lives. I have enough to take care of without making it worse or taking on the troubles or successes of others. This is what Steps Six and Seven contribute to recovery.

Partly to alleviate the guilt I have felt for my past indiscretions and partly because it is the right thing to do, I try to make up for wrongs through restitution, apology, or just being a better person than I was when I drank. Some are old transgressions and some are not retractable, but I do the best I can. I hope this is what Steps Eight, Nine, and Ten ask of me.

In general, I like to be a do-gooder, so I help when and whom I can. This improves my relationships with my community of humans, and it makes me feel good. When I encourage another alcoholic who wants to follow the AA program but doesn't have a clear understanding of higher power, then I am doing Step Twelve.

What is missing? Step Eleven. I have no conscious contact with God—it's just not there and this does not disturb me. I try regularly to train my brain to a more spiritual viewpoint by a practice that includes contemplation, introspection, and affirmation of my gratitude to have been embraced by AA. As a result, I rarely am troubled by that pervasive feeling of separation I used to feel; it has been replaced by a sense of the connectedness of all of us to one other.

Even though I didn't plan it, and even though I don't think about it as "working the Steps," Steps happen in my life as part of an AA-guided recovery. Not one of these practices involves God or believing in God, but all of them together, or each of them alone, fits the intent of the Steps. Atheism and AA's principles are not mutually exclusive, and if anyone tells you that you have to believe in God to stay sober or to remain in AA, he or she is dead wrong. I always tell nonbelievers who ask how they can do those God Steps to look for the goal of the Step and do whatever they can to meet its intent. And don't drink, no matter what happens. Nothing improves if you drink.

*June L.*
*El Granada, California*
*March 2003*

# —To Love Rather Than Be Loved—

When I was drinking, the whole world revolved around me, the Kingpin, or so I thought. I viewed my family members in light of how they helped or hindered my drinking. This perception followed me into recovery. It has taken me over five years of staying sober a day at a time to begin to get an inkling that these family members are individual people with feelings, fears, hopes, and dreams, independent of me.

Sharing around the tables started this awakening. Slowly I came to realize that my AA friends also shared the same daily struggles and successes that I had. But the awakening at home was even slower and more reluctant.

While trying to work the Eighth and Ninth Steps, it was suggested that I demonstrate my willingness to make amends to my husband by saying daily the St. Francis prayer found in the Eleventh Step, inserting my husband's name. I was surprised how unwilling I was to do this, even though I had frequently chanted the refrain of how I wanted our marriage to work. The words of the prayer literally got caught in my throat as I tried to say, "Lord, grant that I may seek rather to comfort my husband than to be comforted by him—to understand my husband, than to be understood by him—to love my husband, than to be loved by him." What? No way! This was all too new. But I used to "act as if" and I continued to say the prayer daily whether I meant it or not. Slowly my attitude softened and I began to see a husband who has the same struggles I have and who needs the same encouragement and love that I want.

Now as I pray and talk to my AA friends, I am learning that I am capable of supplying some of that encouragement and love to my husband. I find that I am clumsy and inconsistent in my encouragement and frequently I feel inadequate and powerless. But that's okay, too. I had thought I was the greatest lover and the supreme caregiver, but I am finding that I know very little about loving and caring. Yet with willingness, prayer, and a sense of humor, I know I can learn how to relate to this man I have lived with for twenty years, but whom I have just begun to really see.

And the children? I thought that would be easy. I've always loved and cared for them, or so I thought. Yet the process was just as surprising and demanding. The words of the St. Francis prayer again stuck in my throat. I found I wanted my kids to comfort me, to understand me, and to love me, more than the other way around. I was shocked. What kind of mother am I? I am not what I thought I was. But with this painful revelation has come the opportunity to listen and learn from my children.

Working the Eighth and Ninth Steps at home has opened my eyes to my family members who have feelings independent of me. I didn't know this before. I thought they all revolved around me, the Kingpin. It is a new freedom to discover that I am no longer the Kingpin, but instead only one in a family of five, all of whom are trying to find their own way in this world. For this I am grateful.

*Joanne L.*
*Madison, Wisconsin*
*March 1990*

# —"How It Works" Works For Me—

As a newcomer, I first heard "How It Works" before I ever picked up a Big Book. It conveyed the essence of the program in a couple of minutes. Its repetition over the years has served as a general reminder. After all, alcoholics have short memories.

Legend has it that Bill W. wrote "How It Works" in approximately forty minutes, his pen flowing across the paper as if taking dictation. Perhaps not. Perhaps he agonized over every phrase, and the early AAs who reviewed his efforts went over every passage with a finetooth comb, debating until dawn.

I don't know. I wasn't there. But I am here today, and I am sober. "How It Works" has been a key part of my sobriety. I have heard it read aloud by people from all walks of life. I have seen its words gestured in American Sign Language, I have seen the blind read it from Braille editions of our Big Book. I have attended large gatherings where an audience of thousands helped the speaker count off each Step as "How It Works" was read from the podium. I have seen people scramble for their reading glasses when the only copy available was someone's wallet-sized card.

I go back to an image I'll never forget from my early days in the program. An old-timer listened to "How It Works" as we began our Saturday morning meeting. Her eyes were closed, her palms flat on the table in front of her. She gave "How It Works" her undivided attention. Yet, how many times had she heard those words in seventeen years of sobriety?

Perhaps for some, "How It Works" has become a tired, overworked bit of dogma, and opportunity to daydream. But not for this alcoholic. I get more out of these words with each passing day. The words don't change, but I do.

*Diana S.*
*Paradise, California*
*October 2003*

---

**From "Simple Truths in an Intellectual Age"—June 1975**

AA gives us a suggested program of Twelve Steps. Their purpose is to teach us how to live a useful, happy life, at peace with ourselves and our fellow human beings. Their purpose is to open our minds and hearts to the greatest happiness we can experience, in helping others, in sharing. Their purpose is to enable us to become spiritually reborn.

The wisdom of AA, however, is so deep that it confines its own part in our personal recovery to nothing more than suggestion. AA leaves it entirely up to you and to me to decide, not only whether to use this program, but also how to use it.

You take your inventory; you clear your inner self of all that is useless and of questionable value. You determine which of your mental con structions are outdated, worthless, ugly obstacles; you order them torn down and junked. And you are the architect, planning the structure of your new, expanding personality right in that clean, fresh-cleared space. You alone decide how deep and wide you want the foundation to be, to anchor the building, and how high its towers shall aim.

—H. M., Newhall, California

—

# A Daily Reprieve

*What we really have is a daily reprieve contingent on
the maintenance of our spiritual condition.*
—Alcoholics Anonymous

Whether or not we go to church or temple regularly, whether our Higher Power is called God or Creative Intelligence or simply the Spirit of the Universe, most AAs agree that ours is a spiritual program. We may not be able to define "spiritual condition" exactly, but we know what the Big Book suggests. It recommends that we give up playing God and trying to control everything and everybody. That we set aside self-centeredness for service. That we make humility, love, and tolerance a part of our lives. And that we practice prayer and meditation in order to connect with a power greater than ourselves, whatever form that might take.

All of us can take comfort in the fact that we don't need an advanced degree in religion to explore and nourish our spiritual life. We need only to become willing to open the door to faith and follow a few suggestions—just for today. Every new day is a fresh page, a new chance to put AA to work. The Big Book puts it simply: "We had to find a power by which we could live—and it had to be a Power greater than ourselves."

# —Hang Gliding—

When I came into AA after twenty-four years of daily drinking, I was ready for a new way of life. My "treatment" was two to three meetings a day at "The Divine Dump" in San Francisco, a long-time meeting place in a neighborhood full of bars and funeral homes. The old-timers would point at these establishments and tell us, "If you don't like it here, try it out there."

For the first three months, I practiced the "ism"—I sponsored myself. But I did ask for help through the emotional storms of early sobriety from the people I saw every day at the meetings. The Steps that everyone spoke about, which hung crookedly on the wall, mystified me. My will had always been my higher power, way before I started to drink; drinking simply helped ease the pain of life not going my way.

I was also an agnostic and cynic. The idea of turning my will and my life over to something other than my own efforts at control was an action that I simply could not imagine. But I wanted this new way of life desperately, so I listened closely to what people had to say in meetings about their experience of coming to believe. Initially, I was repelled by those who talked about God, but they had a joy and a calm that I wanted.

An important part of my coming to believe was spending time at the ocean, where I could see a power greater than myself in action. Several times a week, I would go out to an abandoned WW II fort situated on a bluff overlooking the beach. It was an area for hang gliders, and I'd always enjoyed watching them sail by as I walked along the cliffs and down to the beach. I'd always yearned for the freedom that flight represented. I even had thirty hours of flight logged in small, aerobatic planes before giving it up, as I did with many pursuits during my drinking. As part of my training, I'd learned that the impact of alcohol increases as one ascends into the air, so I usually drank before I flew, to latch on to that thrill.

One day out at the fort, as I was struggling with how to work the Third

Step, I found myself watching the hang gliders as they got ready to launch themselves. They lumbered up to the take-off spot with this heavy equipment on their backs, and then simply stepped into space from this very small spit of sand on the edge of a cliff. This was an intermediate skills area, so everyone had a certain expertise with the principles of aerodynamics. They knew what to do when they left the ground and moved into the air. A week before, however, a man had hesitated as he took off, and he'd fallen down the cliff and died, breaking his neck.

Hearing this story opened up the path to the Third Step for me. I had learned the principles of AA flight from Steps One and Two. I had seen how halfway measures could lead me out of the program to certain death. What I had to do was stand on the edge of the unknown, have faith in the Steps and my teachers in the meetings, and let go—step with both feet into this terrifying new realm of surrender, and trust that a power greater than myself, which I was only coming to understand, would carry me. If I held back, trying to keep one foot in the old realm, I'd fall out of the program. I had to abandon myself absolutely to the principles of the new dimension.

*Bette-B B.*
*Omaha, Nebraska*
*March 2005*

# —Trusting the Silence—

Sometimes my faith in a Higher Power slips. I look at the people, places, and things around me and ask, "Is this really what you had in mind for me? Is this what I sobered up for? Is this all there is?" And I sometimes get the silent treatment. That's only fair. My mouth has usually been running overtime, anyway.

Who is God? I don't need to know. I only need to have faith in a power greater than myself. What matters is what works, not my opinion of what works.

It took me years to figure that out, years in which I did mental and emotional battle with other people's conception of God, years in which I managed only to make myself miserable, cringing or scoffing whenever someone mentioned Steps Three or Eleven. It took me a while sober to realize that it's a waste of time to take God's inventory.

So I don't pretend to know God well. And I really don't claim to pray respectably. I say the words "Thy will, not mine, be done" as if they were magic, as if they could help me stop yammering so much to have my will done. My prayers are usually brief and to the point. "Help!" is one I use often.

Often in sobriety, I've prayed when I needed to meditate. I've yammered at God so much that God can't get a word in edgewise. (What I practice with people, I cannot help but practice with God.) To me, meditation is simply being quiet and listening for a change. It is buttoning up my lip—and my mind that yaps even when my mouth is shut.

Meditation is the path by which I cease being caught up in my own mental "garbage in/garbage out" recycling. It is the path by which I walk out of the turmoil, trouble, pain, depression, and frustration that I create in and around me.

Meditation is when I learn to be a child again. Not a noisy brat, but a child of the sort I always admired but rarely was as a child—quiet, serene, loving, trusting, teachable.

To meditate means I have to become willing to sit alone in silence—and endure silence patiently. It means trusting the silence around me for a while, as if it were an answer I had long sought. This is simple but not easy for me to do. I don't meditate to hear God's voice inside me, but merely to allow some space and time for the awareness of something higher than myself to grow more strongly within me.

I began doing meditation when I gave up my childish habit of expecting God to part the Red Sea and save me from myself once again, when I gave up my spoiled-brat routine of expecting God to show me a burning bush to prove that God really does care about me.

Practicing meditation means I open up for spiritual contact before disaster strikes, before even the need for prayer becomes desperately obvious. It's the brand of spiritual contact with God that I practice early enough in the day that I have nothing to tell God and nothing to ask God about in prayer.

Meditation is the only time when I can be absolutely sure that I am not running on self-will.

In the beginning, while admitting I didn't know the first thing about how to meditate, I turned my ignorance into a major case of self-confusion by reading various books on meditation and trying to follow all the guidelines they presented.

Then simplicity mercifully struck. I found I didn't need to learn how to meditate before meditating. It turned out to be one of those learn-as-you-go things—just as learning how to stay sober is part of staying sober a day at a time. Meditation is something like showing up on a new job I don't know how to do, only to find out that by merely showing up on a regular basis and doing what is placed before me, I'm automatically doing what at first I did not know how to do and was sure I could never do.

When I practice listening in AA meetings, I am learning something I can use in private meditation practice. It took me a while to learn how to really listen to others in AA, to have my mind solely on what the speaker was saying, instead of hearing only the part that plugged me into my own preferred thinking. What I do in meetings is called listening. When I listen alone with God, it is called meditating. When I can listen completely to what you have to say without having to change or criticize it to meet my expectations, then I have a better chance of being able to do the same thing with God the next time I pray or meditate.

The hardest thing for me to do is listen honestly when I've asked God in prayer for direction regarding a particular person, place, or thing. I tend to put words in God's mouth—the ones I want to hear. After years of misunderstanding God, I've devised for myself a simple test for reliability in prayer: If the answer is the one I want to hear—or the one that lets me sit back amid my complacency, laziness, or fear and let someone else do all the work in solving my problem for me—it probably isn't God's answer. What God wants me to do is rarely what I want to do.

For instance, if I want to avoid or leave, God wants me to stay and handle. If I want to be understood or accepted by others, God wants me to try to understand or accept others a bit more. If I want to forget, God wants me to forgive. If I want to point the finger of blame at someone else, God wants me to see my part in creating the disaster. If I want to dislike someone because of a grating character defect he or she has, God wants me to see the same defect in myself.

Meditation not only helps me hear God and others better, it also helps me see how even the tiny things I do daily for others strengthen me in my ability to cooperate with God. For I am one of those hardheaded alcoholics who had to practice cooperating with others for a while to learn how to cooperate with God, so that "turning it over" could become almost as easy and often as automatic as not taking the first drink.

In the last year, I've heard more silence than messages from God while praying or meditating. At this stage in my development, I think God is trying to teach me something I could not learn otherwise about patience and trust. What I'm now learning is how to apply to myself a bit of Native American wisdom that my sponsor shared with me over a decade ago: "If someone comes to you

**From "Miracles: Yours and Mine"—February 2004**

After three months of sobriety, I got drunk. I got good and drunk and good and sick, as usual. Nothing had changed. I couldn't face my sponsor, my family, my group, or worst of all, myself. I couldn't look in the mirror.

A few days later the phone rang. It was that good sponsor—a man dying of cancer and too ill to conduct the AA meeting in a nearby mental institution. Reluctantly, I agreed to chair the meeting. At that time, an outside AA was required to open the meeting. Roughly fifty percent of the patients were there due to chronic alcoholism.

It was not the most joyous meeting I ever chaired, but chair it I did. Then I left, alone, to drive home. It was dark, cold, and snow was falling, and all I could think of was a drink.

I drove a mile or so through the snow and trees to a convenient tavern. I parked in the dark cold, amid the icy puddles. I opened the car door ... and then, shut it. How could I go through all that hell again? But worse, how could I go without a drink! Again, I opened the car door ... and closed it. Then, I sank into despair. Suddenly, I heard a voice; the voice was real, but no one else was there. I wasn't afraid. The voice simply said, "Dave, it never has to be like this again. Go back to AA." That was all.

I started the car and headed home. In the middle of a long bridge over the Susquehanna River, it occurred to me that I had never truly given myself to AA. I decided I would make AA my way of life—whatever that took. I resolved to go to a meeting every evening for a year. I didn't, of course. But I did attend five to six meetings a week, and I stayed sober. Somehow, on that bridge, I felt intense peace—an unreal serenity unlike anything I had ever experienced before. In the years since that parking lot, I have not had one desire to take a drink.

Years later, I was attending a friend's ninth AA birthday. He said that he'd never had a miracle happen. Nothing like Bill's in that hospital. Nothing like the one I had in that parking lot. I said that it seemed to me a huge miracle that he'd stayed sober for nine years! He was clearly shaken. He brightened with the quick realization that that was very much a miracle.

I think we simply fail to recognize miracles for what they are. Sobriety—one-day-at-a-time—is truly a miracle.

—Dave L., Prineville, Oregon

who is hungry and you give that person a fish, that person will expect to get a fish from you every time hunger strikes. But if, when the person comes to you the first time, you teach her or him to fish, that person will never be hungry again." So the messages I receive during meditation or prayer aren't anything like a fish from God. Instead, the messages are like God's lessons in fishing.

Whatever I learn during meditation applies to me in my life, not necessarily to anyone else. The messages are usually what I need to hear at a particular time, whether I agree or not. For example:

Help yourself by helping someone else first.

When in doubt, be silent.

Grow where you are planted.

*Anonymous*
*November 1991*

## —Honoring One's Faith—

My name is David, and I am an alcoholic. I was the last one to know. I can't count how many times I've heard or read someone else say that same thing: "I was the last one to know." But, honestly, I didn't believe that I was an alcoholic, even when I landed in a rehabilitation center. I figured anybody who couldn't drink, for whatever reason, was the poorest sap on the planet. How sad it must be, I thought, to never get drunk. But I soon learned that I didn't drink like other people.

I always seemed to stay close to alcohol. I drank to calm down, to sleep, to celebrate, and to vacation, and I always drank too much. I define "too much" as the point where I throw up and forget what happens next. I know now how foolish I looked.

Everybody was telling me to ease up, but I didn't. I didn't even understand what they were speaking about. I always figured I could stop whenever I wanted to—I just didn't want to. Each time I drank I thought, This time, no one has to know. I'll just drink a little and everyone else will be none the wiser. No repercussions. I can control it.

I couldn't. Then I would do it again with the same results, but having expected different results. I understand that to be a mark of alcoholism.

Things have changed quite a bit over the last years. I wish I could say I haven't used alcohol, or gone out on a bender and had to reset my sobriety date, but I can't. And I wish that bender hadn't set back my spiritual progress and the trust I'd built up with my family and employers, but it did.

However, I can say that I am grateful to the depths of my heart that I now have twenty-one months of sobriety. I am grateful because no more do I hear that I've done something stupid again or ruined a vacation by being soused.

I can look at my kids without the anguish of knowing that I'm affecting their lives negatively any time I'm not working my program. I love my children and they look up to me as their source of strength. I do not have to further jeopardize that because today—one day at a time—I am sober.

Recently, I obtained a lucrative and high position in a company. I was hired the very day I first interviewed. The manager told me that my honesty and frankness impressed him and therefore I would be great for the job. While AA doesn't promise that every member will get a great job by working a program, I surely believe that without a program, I wouldn't have been able to be so open and honest, self-assured, and confident.

As an Orthodox Jew, I was worried that I would not be able to work the Steps. After all, I'm told to get on my knees to pray (which Orthodox Jews do not do) and to say the Lord's Prayer from the New Testament in the Gospel of Matthew (which is uniquely Christian). Some AAs go so far as to tell me to break our holy days to drive to meetings, saying that AA is a spiritual program and I don't need my religion anymore.

I quickly learned that there are many Orthodox Jews in the program. It's not as if we are immune to the disease of alcoholism. We don't get on our knees; we pray in our usual way, and use our religion to boost the spirituality of the program. We pray a silent prayer when the Lord's Prayer is said, or we remain silent. And we get together on our holy days to have meetings that we don't have to drive to.

Also, I am not an island. I go to at least one meeting every day, two on Sunday, and I don't need to stand out like a sore thumb. The group accepts me for who I am, and they respect my adherence to my religious principles. My sponsor fully understands my situation, and there is really no problem at all.

For this, I am most grateful. I am a man of God. I am his creation. Every day I seek to do his will for me and for chances to carry that out. I stand ready to help the person with less time than I, the alcoholic who still suffers, and any person whom I can be of service to with God's help, blessing, and guidance.

I owe a great deal to Alcoholics Anonymous and its members, to a loving and caring God of my understanding, and to the Steps for giving me a better life. I remain grateful, AA: Thanks.

*David M.*
*Los Angeles, California*
*May 2006*

# —The Answer to My Prayers—

I wish you'd shared that with me sooner," my Al-Anon friend said. "I could have saved you a lot of time and trouble." I had just shared with him my recent experiences and also how I had added two verses of my own to the St. Francis Prayer, the prayer AA borrows for our Eleventh Step and quoted in the book *Twelve Steps and Twelve Traditions*.

Several years ago, after "For it is by self-forgetting that one finds. It is by forgiving that one is forgiven. It is by dying that one awakens to eternal life," I had started praying, "It is only by being empty that one is filled. It is only by having nothing that one may have everything." It sounded so good, I don't remember giving a thought to what the answer to my prayer might look like. Then it started being answered, slowly at first and building to a crescendo.

"God help me!" was the first prayer I ever truly said; that one was answered very quickly. I was thirty-five and tired of life, a hopeless alcoholic. I screamed out that first prayer while driving around drunk one day at lunch break. Shortly after that I rear-ended an off-duty cop. Two days later I was in treatment, and three days later I was in an AA meeting. It was my second AA meeting. Eighteen months earlier, I had attended one meeting—drunk. I left with the person who twelfth-stepped me (who was the same person who would later drive me to treatment), and I told her, "I'm not religious. I can do this myself." Of course, I couldn't do it myself and when I asked for God's help (even though I didn't know that was what I was doing), God did help me. Rear-ending an off-duty cop and spending the rest of the day in the drunk tank did not seem like the answer to any prayer at the time, but it was.

I should have known from that experience that my additions to the Eleventh Step prayer would be answered. Now I was telling my Al-Anon friend that since last fall I'd lost the business I'd founded and owned for thirty-one years; I had filed for bankruptcy in the spring; I'd lost my truck and car; I'd lost my job; I'd attempted suicide; and I'd buried my father a week before his birthday on Memorial Day. The week after that, my wife left me and I found out my son was in jail, and now I expected to lose my house. Shall I stop? Was my addition to the prayer being answered? Being empty. Having nothing.

Being filled. Having everything. Thank God! A new job that I absolutely love appeared recently. My daughter offered to take me into her home with her husband and my two grandkids. Her caring and compassion is truly heart-felt. My closest AA friend, who has over fifty years of sobriety and whom I see and talk to every day, has been walking with me through the pain. I have a used subcompact that gets two times the gas mileage of the new truck I lost. My wife left, but we are on good, friendly, and open terms, and I got the dogs. My life is being filled and I have been given everything that I need.

What I have been given and what I'm being filled with is God's grace. It is God's grace that I be able to share my life experience with people who truly care. It's God's grace that I be right-sized. It's God's grace that I face and live in my life's situations without a drink. (My sponsor says the miracle for a guy like me is that I haven't had to take a drink.) It's God's grace that I bear the pain and grow. It's God's grace that I am me and live one day at a time ("Un día a la vez," has always been my favorite AA slogan).

The most recent revision I've made to my daily prayers is to change my addition to the St. Francis Prayer to, "It is only by living one day at a time that one may be filled with your grace." I also think more about what I'm praying for and try to be more attuned to the answers that may come. Every day, I ask the God of my understanding, "Let me be responsible, use my experience, find balance, express your will, and help others. For it is by doing these things and helping others that I am helped." I pray I can stay the course as the answers come.

*Skitch F.*
*Albuquerque, New Mexico*
*November 2005*

# —A God Of My Understanding—

When we enter the world of recovery, we are in a sense reborn. During this process, many of us find a need to recreate our concept of a Higher Power, or to build upon the remnants of an existing faith. How and what encompasses a Higher Power? And in what way must one's faith adhere to the structure of the program of Alcoholics Anonymous?

I'd like to share my experience on this topic. I'm originally from India and hail from an orthodox caste known as Brahmins, a class of Hindu priests and religious scholars. My family was traditional and religious in a gentle way. In my childhood years, a sense of confidence in his faith allowed my father to encourage me to read great books of religion. He urged that I not compare, but rather find unity in the essence of all great faiths. At the same time, my parents demonstrated Hindu traditions and philosophies by example. Years later, this subtle approach would prove to be my saving grace.

I had some very profound realizations in early sobriety. I noted how very Christian the program of AA was. The format, collecting money in the baskets, fellowship, and the coffee afterward all contributed to this. Temple services had none of these dynamics. I suppose Hinduism is a very autonomous faith and a need for community is attained largely through the extended family. While I was infinitely more comfortable with the latter, I tapped into my upbringing and "kept an open mind." The Lord's Prayer was another challenge; however, I choose to see this prayer as generous and all-encompassing, guiding me through the day's hardships.

Another obstacle was the concept of "Thy will, not mine, be done" which is very much the antithesis to the Hindu prayer. Hindus specifically pray for one's wishes to be heard. We are encouraged to put our "intention" out to the universe to give confidence to its manifestation. My struggle with adjusting to this difference between the two cultures prompted a desire to delve deeper into the intricacies of my religion. As I studied prayer and intention, I unearthed concepts in the Law of Detachment. I continued to put my intention out to the universe, but detached from the results. I grew to trust that my prayers were indeed answered, regardless of the shape of their manifestation. Contrary to popular belief, Hinduism is a monotheistic religion. The confusion lies in our philosophy and adaptation of a belief that God is everywhere and in everything: Creation—Brahma; Abundance—Lakshmi; Preservation—Vishnu; Destruction—Shiva; Loyalty—Rama and Sita. The list is vast and complex, but the approach is simple in that it helps one comprehend God's omnipresence. A favorite of mine is Ganesh—the remover of obstacles. In sobriety I've found much comfort in praying to this "God."

Incorporating my faith was a difficult process, but I learned more about my religion and was better able to practice the principles of AA to ensure sobriety. It was a worthwhile effort, as my willingness was soon rewarded with occasional but profound experiences with God.

When I became sober, I recall having a magnificent moment of clarity while reading the Twelve Steps posted on a wall. Except for Step One, where "We admit we are powerless over alcohol and our lives have become unmanageable," I realized that the remaining Eleven Steps embody the very philosophy which my forefathers and the pillars of my community adhered to as a way of life. Relief and a sense of safety overcame me. Despite years of spiritual turmoil which alcoholics know too well, I had found the path homeward.

I once heard that the one thing all alcoholics have in common is that they've longed for God. I love that. Today, after years of being lost, I have a deep and unyielding faith in a God that I've always searched for. I believe it's the same faith that my ancestors experienced.

In Hinduism, it is said that all roads to Nirvana, or spiritual actualization, can be reached only through a vehicle—a golden chariot that comes in the form of a saint, guru, teacher, or philosophy. Given the constraints of self, one cannot attain that state unaccompanied. It's amazing to me that this vehicle has come to me—a Hindu Brahmin woman—in the form of the program of Alcoholics Anonymous.

I believe now that the program of Alcoholics Anonymous and its Twelve Steps are divinely inspired. I thank God for bringing me to Alcoholics Anonymous, but mostly I thank Alcoholics Anonymous for bringing me to God.

*Aruna A.*

*Toronto, Ontario*

*March 2006*

# —I Can't Fly That Kite Today—

I am forty-nine years old. As far as I can remember, I never drank responsibly. Through college and my early years of marriage, when I drank, I drank to get drunk. My drinking was always to excess and always dangerous.

Like many adult children of alcoholics, I vowed not to become my father. He died a couple of years ago after a life of alcohol abuse. I can never remember a time growing up when I did not see my father either drinking or drunk. Whenever he got plastered, he started picking on me. It affected me and I developed a deep resentment of my dad.

In 1994, after several dry years, a single drink in a Los Angeles hotel turned into four long years of disaster. My career and family were gone. My reputation in the community was shot. Three rehabs did not help. I was at that hopeless state. I had become just like my dad, with one big exception. I was at least open to Alcoholics Anonymous.

I attended meetings on and off, between sprees. There was something blocking real sobriety. After losing another job, I was drunk again and more hopeless than ever.

A man I met at a meeting came to visit me. He sat and talked with me about his experiences. As he heard my story, he said something shocking. He said I was agnostic! Impossible. You see during those dry years, I accomplished a lot. In addition to becoming the vice president of the local affiliate of a national TV network, I also developed my faith. I went to seminary and earned a master's degree in theology and a doctorate in biblical studies. Agnostic? Never. I had a relationship with God. I read the Old Testament in Hebrew and the New Testament in Greek. How could I be agnostic? Yet as I listened and searched my heart, I knew he was right.

I was agnostic in one sense. I did not believe that a power greater than myself would help me. I had concluded that my alcoholism after so many dry years was a lapse of faith that God would not forgive. I was struggling with the Second Step of our program.

I marvel now when I read "How it Works" in the Big Book. I marvel at the wisdom of including one small word in the explanation of the Second Step. It's a familiar passage,

1. That we were alcoholic and could not manage our own lives
2. That no human power could have relieved our alcoholism
3. That God could and would if he were sought.

God could relieve my alcoholism. I knew that. But I did not believe he would. I was sure I had crossed a line. I was no longer able to appropriate that power to help. But AA stressed that he "would." The original manuscript was even more emphatic: "God can and will!" I was humbled.

My friend pointed out that as I held onto that belief that God "would not" help me, I was showing a kind of spiritual pride. Surely I was worse than any other alcoholic. Surely I was beyond help.

My turning point came when I was, as the Big Book suggests, "convinced." I was convinced that God could and would relieve my alcoholism. I began to take small steps back to that power greater than myself. The first step was to start my day on my knees asking God to keep me sober. It has worked one day at a time.

But my friend pointed out there was a lot more to do. He joined me on his knees as I prayed a Third Step prayer. Then I had to face that Fourth Step and that tremendous resentment toward my dad. That was hard.

With the support and guidance of my friend, who became my closest friend and my sponsor, I set out to deal with resentment, selfishness, and fear. I followed the outline in the Big Book, looking at where and how this resentment toward my dad developed.

I saw that time when I was eight when Dad, a friend, and I were out flying a kite. Dad as usual was drinking. No matter how hard I tried I could not get that kite airborne! My friend, who was much more athletic than I, ran faster and the kite soared. I remember my dad's words, which cut right to my heart and soul: "Sometimes I wish he were my son instead of you." I was crushed. I carried that moment for forty-one years.

The Fourth Step helped me see that moment in a new light. My dad was sick, sick with the disease of alcoholism. I understood firsthand how alcoholism affects a person and the family. I asked my spiritual father to relieve me of anger toward my dad. The kite incident and others brought so much to the surface—each time I faced resentment and fear.

I did my Fifth Step with my sponsor-friend. I faced fear. The fear that held me tight for all these years was a fear that my dad did not love me. I faced that fear with many tears. It was so consuming I knew that no human power could help. I needed a power greater than myself to help. I needed to ask for that help through the Sixth and Seventh Steps.

I finished my Fifth Step about midnight and set my alarm for 5:00 A.M., when I knew it would be quiet, to review my work and "know God better." It was a tremendous spiritual experience. As I reviewed my resentments and fears, it became clear that as I feared my earthly father did not love me, I also had come to believe that my heavenly father did not love me. I had. Here was the source of that agnosticism. For all these years, I had a conception of God based on a life of fear, a life of resentment. I shed tears again. This time I asked my heavenly father to forgive me and to help me to trust him and know him. Years of heaviness were lifted.

I still begin my day with prayer, and when I feel overwhelmed by events or circumstances, I often find myself whispering a prayer that goes something like this, "Father in heaven, I just can't seem to fly that kite today. Please help me." And my experience, strength, and hope is that he does.

*Frank A.*
*Scranton, Pennsylvania*
*April 2002*

# Letting Go of Old Ideas

*... we find that bit by bit we can discard the old life—the one that did not work—for a new life that can and does work under conditions whatever.*
—Bill W., The Greatest Gift of All, AA Grapevine, December 1957

As active drinkers, we were often plagued by fear, self-pity, loneliness, resentment, and hopelessness; we saw our place in the world through a cloud of negativity. The worst-case scenario was the script of our lives. In sobriety, we find that those old ideas don't serve us. As a result of attending meetings, engaging in prayer and meditation, doing Step work, accepting service jobs big or small, our habits of thinking and doing begin to change. We realize we can make choices that bring us happiness and peace of mind instead of simply stewing in our misery.

In this section, AA members describe how they made new choices—looked for solutions instead of problems, replaced knee-jerk negativity with a positive outlook, traded fear for hope. The great promise of Alcoholics Anonymous, beyond the promise of sobriety, is that change is possible for each one of us. From being stuck in an alcoholic muddle we can go to the fresh possibilities of hope.

# —The Two-Letter Word—

THE CHILDHOOD MEMORY THAT made the biggest impression on me was being scolded for repeating a "four-letter" word. I still have an occasional slip of the tongue, but I think there is one word that no alcoholic should ever repeat—a word so damaging that it has every right to take its place alongside even the harshest of four-letter words. This word is "if."

For example, each sober morning, I usually wake up in a good frame of mind. But let's say I happen to pass by the bathroom mirror, and come to the conclusion that "if I lost some weight, I'd look better." While getting ready for work, I might decide that "if I had a better job, I'd be happier." Instantly, I start to feel my once positive mood begin to curdle.

I've discovered that when I'm saying the word "if" what I'm really saying, on a subconscious level, is "I wish." And when I start wishing for things, my focus shifts from all the things I have to be grateful for to everything I think I want—or deserve! Then, just like the old adage about seeing a glass of water as being either half empty or half full, nothing in my life seems good enough. By continuing to follow through with this hazardous train of thought, I could very well "if" myself right back to the nearest barstool.

In short, I now understand that just as I have no mental defense against taking that first drink, I also have no mental defense against speaking that first "if." Just as one drink will lead to another, one "if" will lead to another, until I am awash in a sea of negativity. The only thing that might look good to me at this point would be a drink. I learned at a young age that when I said a four-letter word, I expected to pay certain consequences. I think the same goes for saying "if." Only, in this instance, instead of having my mouth washed out with soap, the price I pay is the loss of my serenity. Fortunately, AA has taught me that I have choices. There are actions I can take to derail this debilitating mental process. First, I can ask the God of my understanding to relieve me of this burden. Next, I can talk to my sponsor or call another trusted AA friend who will most likely advise me to make out a gratitude list. But nothing seems to help me more than being reminded where I came from, and the kind of person I used to be while under the influence of alcohol—that sad, fearful, undependable sort of person I will become again, unless I start to focus on my needs instead of my wants.

*Tracey B.*
*Williamstown, West Virginia*
*December 2001*

# —Turning Points—

*Half measures availed us nothing. We stood at the turning point. We asked His protection and care with complete abandon.*

— Alcoholics Anonymous

When I first came to Alcoholics Anonymous, I didn't know that I wanted what you people had; I just knew that I was sick and tired of what I had. So, I figured there must be something to what I heard around the rooms of AA, even though it sounded like psychobabble. Your sayings and expressions didn't make sense to me. A couple of them in particular kept pounding at my head: "If you want your life to change, you have to change your life" and "If you keep doing what you always did, you keep getting what you always got." I knew my life needed to change, but how? Even with all my crazy thinking, somehow I knew that God could accomplish these things in my life. Alone, I had no clue.

I was given the idea in AA meetings that I would have to start getting honest. This idea scared me to death. I had always lied—to you, to everyone—but especially to myself. So just trying to be honest in everything I did and said would be a full-time job. How could I do all that and still not drink? But with my Higher Power to guide me, I "honestly" tried to implement this principle into my life. If I caught myself in even the most miniscule lie, I would stop and say out loud, "No, that is a lie," and then proceed with the truth. And I put a sign on my bathroom mirror that said, "You are looking at the problem."

If my life was going to change, I knew that my thinking needed to change. I had had stinking thinking my entire life. How was I supposed to change that? The answer came at an AA meeting: "You have to live yourself into better thinking; you can't think yourself into better living." I know now that God was the one who gave me a different way to start living and eventually new and different ideas. I knew that there was no way I could have come up with some of the thoughts that were coming into my mind. One incident especially still reminds me how my thinking began to differ.

Early in sobriety, I was a single mom, going to college in a nearby town. This particular winter afternoon, coming home from school, I decided to take a less-traveled two-lane highway, instead of my usual route of the heavily-traveled interstate. When I was about halfway home, my rear tire blew out. I easily pulled off the road and began to change the tire. Instead of my old thought processes that would have cursed God for the flat tire and the cold weather, my immediate thought was "Thank you, God, that I have a spare, that I am a woman who knows how to change a flat, that I am safe on this less-traveled road, and that this blow-out did not happen while I was driving eighty miles an hour on the interstate." Oh my gosh! Where did these thoughts come from? This certainly was not my old way of thinking; these were actually prayers of thanksgiving.

I also learned that I had to get rid of slippery people, places, and things in my life; that they would lead to slips. The first test of many to come was one night when I was about four or five months sober. There was a knock on my apartment door very late at night. My children had gone to their dad's for the weekend and I was alone. I went to the window and looked out, but I could see no vehicle. It didn't feel right and I was afraid. The knock came again; I said, "Who is it?" A voice came back "It's me, Ken." Ken had been an old drinking buddy of my ex-husband and mine. I opened the door a

---

**From "The Gift of Powerlessness" – December 1992**

Recently gratitude has taken on a deeper meaning. The whole concept of gratitude depends upon receiving a gift. We are grateful for the gift, and express our gratitude through actions toward others. But what does it mean to receive a gift? For me, a gift is something I receive through no merit of my own. For something to be a gift, it must be freely given with no strings attached. Things that I earn or deserve cannot be gifts.

It is in that sense that I call sobriety a gift. There were many times when I said, "This is my last drink," but it was not. Finally a time came when I gave up, and in my defeat, found that I no longer had the compulsion to drink. This freedom was not of my doing, it was nothing that I had earned or deserved. I can only view it as a gift.

Now when I review my gratitude list, I see that it consists of things that were not brought about by my efforts. Time and again I discover that when I stop trying to force things my way, the natural outcome turns out wonderful. When I stay out of the way, my whole life unfolds like a gift. All I need do is rely on the gift giver—my Higher Power.

—Jim B., San Jose, California

---

crack and said, "Ken, it's very late. What do you want?" "I've got cold beer and some weed. Thought you'd want to party." "No, I don't drink anymore." "Yeah," he retorted, "I heard, but just have one drink with me. Then I'll leave." "No, Ken, go home. I'm not interested. It's late." I stuck to my guns, and he stood there persistently trying to pull me back into the gutter. Finally he got on his motorcycle (that was why I didn't see a car) and left. "Thank you, God," I spoke the words out loud, "that I did not say 'Yes, come on in,' or 'Sure, just one drink.'" I guess the word gets around in a small town, because after a while, the partyers didn't knock on my door anymore. My old fair-weather friends found me boring. They had no idea that I was having more fun than I had ever had in my life!

Financial problems began to ease up a bit. Being honest meant I had to take care of rent and other bills before I could buy clothes or go out to eat.

Before, I went to the liquor store with my paycheck first; the other necessities of life, like groceries and rent, had to wait. I had to drink first. Now here I was, sober and a single parent living below the poverty line. Yet somehow, I managed to purchase a car from my parents, and pay it off. I was never late with a rent check; the refrigerator and the cabinets were full of food. The heat and air conditioner worked; we took hot baths and I paid the bills. My kids and I may not have had everything we wanted, but we were blessed with lots of things that I knew were directly in proportion to my not drinking and trying to live according to God's will instead of my own.

Now, after nine years of trying to live God's way instead of my own, I still stand at the turning point each and every day. I wake up and decide what kind of person I will be. Will I arise with blessings for another beautiful day, or will I mumble that I must get up and go to that darn job? Will I snap harshly at my family, or will I listen intently and speak softly? Will I go to meetings, read my Big Book, talk to my Higher Power, and listen? Or will I neglect these things and forget that they have given me a new life? Do I forget to thank God at night for another sober day? Do I remember that I am a drunk and that not drinking and just attempting to work and live the Twelve Steps means that I am a miracle? Yes, every day I stand at the turning point. I am just one stinking thought away from a drink, and I am just one drink away from death. God is truly doing for me what I could not do for myself.

*Sunny H.*
*Bald Knob, Arkansas*
*March 2004*

# —How Is My Now?—

Well, I'm a half-century old now, and I have decided to face the music and become a grown-up. That word was uttered during my youth with such reverence: "When I get big enough, I can sit at the dining room table with

> **From "Circles Of Sobriety"—January 2006**
>
> I am allergic to alcohol and must not put it into my digestive system. If I protect my thinking, I'm able to stay dry. If I consistently think grateful, logical, rational, positive thoughts, then my emotions, which stem in part from my thinking, will reflect those thoughts.
>
> It's important to monitor my thinking, to be conscious of what thoughts I'm hugging to my heart, inviting to stay in my mind, encouraging to hang around my head.
>
> Tough? Yes, but not being aware of what I'm thinking can allow my thinking to run the whole show: emotions, decisions, and actions. Dry drunk, here I come!
>
> Serenity protects my thinking, and everyone's recipe for serenity is different. It's like vegetable soup—nobody makes it quite the same. It can even vary from day to day, depending on what's left over in the fridge. For me, serenity means getting enough sleep, eating the right food, and staying out of other folks' business. Everyone has her or his own formula.
>
> Easy? Absolutely not, but far more worth the expenditure of energy than what went into recovering from hangovers.
>
> —Francis G., Chestertown, New York

the grown-ups," we children would say wistfully at family gatherings.

And I suppose it's finally time. Taking responsibility for my own actions and behaviors isn't something I relish doing. It's so much easier for me to continue being the victim, thus justifying my bad behaviors: you did this to me or you said that to me or you did it to me first. And on and on and on.

The AA program has taught me that changed behaviors are simple but not easy. I may know exactly what change I need to make but actually making it can be difficult. It takes commitment, tenacity, and a level of faith that the change itself will result in good. I'm learning that from AA people. I watch those I respect; I watch their calm demeanor, their ability to act responsibly, their commitment to a spiritual way of life that has allowed them to walk through pain and come out the other side with a smile still on their faces as they utter the words, "I am so grateful to be here today to live this wonderful life."

I borrowed others' faith for a long time, and now I'm beginning to get a bit of my own. I wake up most mornings with a feeling of positive anticipation for what the new day will bring. I look forward to participating in my life, whereas in the past I was always waiting for something to happen before I could get on with this business of living. I spent my entire life getting ready to live. And it seemed there was always just one more thing that needed to happen before I could consider doing that.

I used to lament over and over the things that didn't go right for me yesterday, last week, last year, or when I was a child. Meanwhile, I carefully mapped out my plans for things that would have to be done tomorrow, next week, or the rest of my life. I was so busy juggling the regrets of the past with the expectations of tomorrow I had no time for living in the present. I missed those precious moments of today.

No more. I am living in the moment. I am participating in my life as it happens today. If my neighbor invites me over for coffee when I'm in the midst of baking a cake, I ask her to come to my house and visit while I'm working. If a friend calls in need of support, I stop watching the ball game on television and listen to her. If my husband suggests an impromptu movie on a Sunday afternoon, I allow myself to alter my plans and go. In the past, everything had to be scheduled, had to be on the list, or it couldn't be considered. I still make those lists each day but now with the understanding that changes—even deletions—are real options. I believe my to-do lists give me focus, but I do not believe (as I used to) that they are written in stone. If the kitchen drawer doesn't get cleaned out, but I get a much-needed midday nap instead, that's okay today. I did the more important thing.

A dear friend gave me a phrase some years ago that I often use. When I find myself consumed with regrets for the past or wallowing in fears for the future, I ask myself, "But how is my now?"

And you know what? My now is really awfully good. I am alive and physically well; I have a loving family, countless good friends, and a spiritual way of life today that allows me to participate in my own life as a responsible grown-up. And now I'm able to say, "I am so grateful to be here today to live this wonderful life."

*Barb G.*
*Atlanta, Georgia*
*August 2001*

# —A Walk Through the Day, Drunk and Sober—

My gratitude should start as soon as I wake up, but I am a human being so it takes a shower and a coffee or two to ignite the sparks. I never considered myself a slow learner, just a fast forgetter. But I'm grateful I can get up today and not lie in bed playing dead, worrying if it's safe to come out.

So we're up and breakfasted. Another miracle, first meal of the day going down and staying down, then a kiss, not a scowl, from my wife before she leaves for work. Ten minutes yet before I leave. Coffee, silence, and the reading for that particular day fill the void. May be the only bit of serenity I get all day, so it's well-savored. I usually try to guess just how many mistakes I'm going to make that day. I always allow for at least forty-five.

Now which jacket to wear? Grateful I have more than one to choose from today. Didn't even have one when I went to my first meeting. Left them all in bars, which I elected to leave in a hurry. Daniel never went back into the Lion's Den to see whether he left his work cap and neither did I!

Then it's chin up and without thinking, straight out the front door. Not like the old days when it was collar up and sneak out the back door and over the fence, through the woods, down the embankment, along the railway, over the wall, up the street, and into the darkened, smoke-filled bar before someone sees you. What a way to spend a bright, sunny summer's day.

Now to the car, which is legally parked right outside and starts first time. Never crossed my mind it wouldn't. In the old days, it would be parked up the nearest hill, facing Mecca with the jump leads in the glove compartment just in case. Always puzzled me that there I was, one alcoholic workaholic and still the last owner of every car I ever owned. If the truth be told, I never should have possessed a license anyway, and am grateful that I have one today. So we're off to work. Yes, legitimate work. Not full-time casual, but honest-to-goodness paid employment. There's a traffic jam on the bridge. I'm going to be late. No point getting worried or upset about it. There must be 150 cars in the same queue, so we all share a 150th of the stress. It's not just something "that always happens to me." It happens to everyone, so I'll shut up and be patient. My boss, my colleagues, and the office cat are not "out to get me"; it's only my head that's "out to get me." No one ever got sacked for being unavoidably late.

Into work, give and receive "good mornings," then head down and get on with it at a steady pace. And no heart attacks when the door behind you opens. It's not the "We've-found-you-out police" coming to expose my murky deeds from last weekend. It's my mate to see if I need help with anything. Am I man enough to accept? Or will I say, "Everything is fine, I can manage" when I'm really out of my depth? Many hands make light work. The offer is gratefully accepted.

The working day goes by as it does for everyone in the country. Some good, some not so, but this is where the program of AA is designed to be worked. You can't live in AA meetings; they can only prepare you for life the way it was always meant to be lived. You don't build a ship to leave it in the dry dock, so you have to attend meetings to equip yourself for whatever sunshine or storms life throws your way. If it's not all going my way, then it must be going the right way.

Lunchtime is here, so I'm off to the canteen and sit where I please. I no longer sneak away into a corner and put a newspaper on the seat next to me so I don't have to talk anyone. Some folks have even kept me a seat! The soup looks good, and my hands are steady enough to eat it without spraying it all over the table. Proper food instead of alcohol for lunch—no wonder my body took ages to heal. When you start replacing nutritious food with the poison of booze, you've got a real problem on your hands. Good food and healthy conversation, what a difference. If you want a healthy body, you have to be careful what you put in it. The requirements for a healthy mind are just the same. Be watchful of your intake.

Back to work for the rest of a productive day; then it's off home. Using the front door again; twice in one day—would have been impossible before.

A pile of mail behind the door gets opened right away, no hiding some down my trousers and scrutinizing the rest before I decide not to open any. Previously each piece of mail was treated like a letter bomb. Don't touch it and you won't get hurt. Two drinks later it would be "What right has the government to send me such letters anyhow? Don't they know who I am?"

The mail all sorted, it's off to a meeting, taking the new kid on the block. He's coming along nicely. He can't see it, but everyone else can. In a way recovery is like the illness, the person it affects most is always last to notice, last to lift up his head and look the world in the eye. Any fool can put up a hand and admit wrong; it takes real courage to forgive yourself and get on with living the life you were always meant to be living.

Back home, a bit tired. The program promised me peace, not rest. My wife and I have a good chat about our respective days, our kids, and our plans. A day at a time applies to my emotional life. I still want to use my newfound freedom to the full, and this takes careful planning.

Just the two of us in the home now, and it is a home, not just a place to crash between drinking bouts. Kids all grown up and out of the nest. They say an alkie's kids are like flowers that never open until the booze is removed from their lives. Only then do they turn into something beautiful.

Then it's another shower and into my own bed at the usual time, another miracle. Read a few pages of a good book before putting out the light. The brain is now clear enough to read books with more than two characters in them! My bookmark has a Step Ten inventory printed on it. A spot check to remind me I'm only human. Can't find anything that would keep me awake;

something must be working. Never even told a lie. Then again, even back when I only told one, it was the one I used all the time: "It wasn't me!"

With the most sincere gratitude, I thank my God it's not like that today, and there is no need for it to be like that tomorrow if I stick with this simplest of programs. Gratitude is not a word in AA. It's an action.

*Oakley John*
*Cumbernauld, Scotland*
*June 2003*

# —Down From the Mountaintop—

I woke up with my last hangover on July 5, 1988, and found my way into a meeting of Alcoholics Anonymous in San Francisco a few days later. After a few months, it became clear that there were people in AA who laughed, and had a life, and they were usually talking about the Steps and sponsorship and service. So I bought a Twelve-Step workbook. The workbook was okay as far as it went, but I skipped through the God stuff. I had been raised an atheist and hadn't yet realized that it took as much faith to be an atheist as to be a believer. I also skipped getting a sponsor. I had spent fifty years building walls around myself and pushing people away; I wasn't about to get chummy with anyone. Consequently, when I got to Step Five, I had a bit of a dilemma, so I thought I might do a sort-of Fifth Step with my wife in hopes of saving our marriage. But there were a couple of things I wasn't sure I wanted to tell her, so at eight months sober, I actually asked someone at a meeting for advice, and by the end of that conversation, asked him to be my sponsor. He agreed, and I said, "I'm ready for Step Five." He said, "C'mon over Saturday and let's look at Step One."

That began an extraordinary journey. I embraced the Steps (except for the God stuff) and found them liberating. I got to see who I was and where I came from, that I wasn't a freak dropped from outer space (although there was a period when I would have welcomed alien abduction). However, I did leave out one little thing in my Fifth Step, that most deeply shaming thing I couldn't yet talk about, and by chiseling on the Steps I missed having that spiritual awakening the Twelve Steps are meant to evoke. So my second year sober was a roller coaster; I was acting out in ways crazier than when I was drinking. The Higher Power I didn't believe in was trying to get my attention, big time! I developed a nervous tic in one eye, had chronic neck and back pain, had a panic attack while driving and had to pull off the road, dreamed I was in a plane that was crashing and dreamed I was drinking at an AA meeting and hiding the bottle under the table. I talked to another alcoholic about it and said I was afraid I was heading for a relapse.

"You've already had the relapse," he said. "You just haven't picked up the drink yet." That got my attention, and I began several months of intensive work. I told my sponsor the thing I'd left out of my Fifth Step the year before, only to find that he didn't remember my Fifth Step. Talk about ego deflation! I journaled, went to more meetings, and did something I would have laughed at not long before, which turned out to be "inner child" work with a therapist—powerful stuff. I also told myself affirmations, went to a treatment facility for a two-week "tune-up," and ended the summer of 1990 in the Eastern Sierra's White Mountains. I created my own "letting go" ritual, fasting for two days at 14,000 feet, burying things that represented past aspects of my life I wanted to leave behind, and crying my eyes out in the brilliant morning sun.

I came down the mountain changed. I was ready to take actions that would point my life in new directions without my knowing what the outcome would be, or even where I would be living. I came down ready to take that leap of faith, believing that things would work out. I'd had my spiritual awakening and let go of the controls. I had a Higher Power, and it wasn't me. Al, the name I'd used most of my life, stayed on the mountain, and Albert came down, ready to be a whole person.

I went to an AA meeting in Bishop and, for the first time, knew I could go anywhere and find people who would know me and welcome me. I even went to a demolition derby at the county fair and felt as one with the drunks cheering on car crashes! For the first time in my life, I felt human.

Since then, I have continued to use the Steps, do service, have a sponsor and sponsor others, and thank my Higher Power, (whom I don't particularly need to define) for my full and wonderful life. I have maintained serenity through divorce, marriage, another divorce, a benign brain tumor, a clogged artery, and hemorrhoids; I gave up my high school-dropout status, earned three university degrees, and published two books. I've tried tap dancing, cello and saxophone playing. I have remained open to the ongoing wow of life around me, and, at age sixty-five, have fallen head-over-heels in love with a woman who loves me.

Perhaps the greatest gift of sobriety is that ability to love and be loved, connected to the Higher Power who accepts me just as I am and, through he/she/them/it, enables me to accept people just as they are, and they are pretty wonderful.

*Albert L.*
*Tucson, Arizona*
*August 2003*

# —Lemons and Lemonade—

When I first came into AA, few things boiled my blood more than sayings like "When life gives you lemons, make lemonade." I hated a lot of things as a drinker, and positive thinking was at the top of the list.

Out of all the positive-thinking people who shared, I was most annoyed by the ones dealing with their DUI experiences. "It was the best thing that ever happened to me," a woman once said at my regular Sunday morning discussion meeting. One old-timer speaking at my home group said, "I am so grateful to that police officer for arresting me that I send him a card every year on my anniversary and thank him." Over and over, I heard people claim that their DUI arrests were blessings bestowed upon them by their loving Higher Power. These people, I thought, arms crossed over my chest, are either liars or idiots. If arrests are blessings, please shower me with curses.

Over the six weeks between my first AA meeting and my court date, my attitude started to change. I went to meetings, got a sponsor and a home group, and read the literature. I went without a drink for days, weeks, and then over a month, and I started to allow a positive little thought to creep into my head—maybe, just maybe, it was a good thing that I got caught. I needed the wake-up call before something much worse happened.

Then one day I was at a speaker meeting and a man stood up and explained how he had come to AA right after getting arrested for what would have been—if he were convicted—his third DUI. "I really worked the pro-

---

**From Happy Or Unhappy? It's My Call—April 2001**

I'm as happy as I make up my mind to be" is a phrase I've heard at meetings from time to time. Usually, the person who utters it appears to be calm and content, someone who has accepted his or her circumstances and is unwilling to let a situation get him or her down.

In the past, the phrase has been a source of irritation for me. I took it as an indictment of me, my sobriety, and my life. When I heard those words, I heard, "It's your fault if you're not happy." I felt as if the speaker were talking about me instead of about his or her experience, strength, and hope.

Living sober one day at a time, I have come to a different understanding of this phrase. I now understand that I have a choice: I can choose how to react to a situation and choose how I let it affect me. This is not to say I don't have problems. I do. But my problems are my problems—nothing more, nothing less. They are real and I need to deal with them, but they are not who I am. They do not define me.

Am I as happy as I make my mind up to be? Today, I say yes.

—Pearl S., San Leandro, California

gram," he said, "and my Higher Power rewarded me because when I went to court I got off on a technicality."

That's it, I thought. It all made sense to me. I was well on my way to exceeding ninety meetings in ninety days. I had read the Big Book twice. I even had a coffee commitment. How could my Higher Power not come and bail me out? That had to be my reward for sobering up and working a good program.

My sponsor cautioned me. He pointed out the page in the Big Book where it mentions that we are still accountable for the mistakes we made while drinking. Sobriety, he said, doesn't remove accountability. He also mentioned the Third Step, and the idea that I should be doing what was right without expecting anything in return. "We don't pray for things," he said, quoting the literature, "but only for the knowledge of [God's] will for us and the power to carry that out."

I heard him, but didn't really listen. I preferred the idea that my Higher Power would conjure up a technicality and get me off for the DUI. It happened for that other guy, I reasoned. Why not for me?

Then, on the day of my court appearance, my lawyer told me that the prosecutor had me dead to rights and urged me to plead guilty. "If you plead guilty, the judge will go easier on you," he said. "If you don't, he probably won't."

I didn't argue. I knew I was guilty, and it looked after all like my Higher Power would not intervene. No miraculous technicality had appeared to save me from the consequences of my actions. I plead guilty and got my sentence.

That night, at my regular discussion meeting, it seemed that everyone had some joy to share. One man spoke about getting his family back after quitting alcohol. A woman talked about buying her first house. Another gushed over the fact that she'd just landed her dream job. Finally, a guy with time addressed me and the rest of the newcomers. "I used to be like you," he said. "I had nothing. I was miserable. Now, I have a big house, a car, and a beautiful family, all because I work a good program."

I could feel my face turning red with anger, my head starting to pound. I wanted to say that sometimes people worked good programs and didn't get material rewards, but when the leader called on me I started spouting lies. "I am really glad I came tonight," I said. "It's great to hear how well everyone is doing. It gives me a lot of hope."

I went home and stewed, feeling the same angry, betrayed feeling I had always felt toward my Higher Power. Other people were being showered with blessings, and I had to pay the DUI fines and live without a license for six months. Where were the joys of sobriety for me?

I started riding my bike to work each morning—it was a ten-mile round trip—and I couldn't help but notice how reckless and dangerous so many of the drivers seemed. "But they," I thought, angrily directing my thoughts toward my Higher Power, "never have to suffer any consequences for their actions." Morning after morning, I left convinced that I would probably get hit by a truck and become paralyzed, and then I would spend the rest of my life in a wheelchair, listening to happy people tell me about the lemons and the lemonade.

I wallowed in my anger and resentment, though I knew it was both irrational and dangerous. Irrational because I knew I was guilty and deserved the punishment I had received. Dangerous because I had read in the Big Book that resentment sent more people out on drinking binges than anything else.

I started telling people how I really felt before, during, and after meetings. "I haven't gotten anything from sobriety," I would say. "My life sucks more now than it did when I was drinking." The answers I got all came down to about the same thing: You're right where you ought to be. Don't drink and go to meetings. It gets better.

At one beginner's meeting, I told the leader that I didn't really believe in Step Three, turning our lives and our wills over to a Higher Power. I pointed to the crucifix on the wall in the church classroom we used for our meeting. "Jesus said 'thy will be done,' and look what happened to him." The leader told me that I should pray for acceptance. I asked him if he had heard me when I had told him that I didn't trust God. He told me he had once felt the same way and that prayer had worked for him. "Try it," he said.

Try it? I didn't have any better ideas, so I began to pray as I rode my bike to work—or I tried to pray. At first, my prayers would often dissolve into angry screeds, with me once again railing against God.

Gradually, I found myself more and more making the trip in a state of serenity, repeating the Lord's Prayer and the Serenity Prayer, or sometimes thinking about people I knew who seemed to be suffering and asking that God remove their suffering. Because I had to get up so early to pedal to work, I started to notice the sunrise, and—peddling along the streets, rocks popping under my wheels—the flaming colors of fall leaves all around me. One particularly beautiful morning a thought popped into my head: This sure beats waking up with a hangover.

I lost fifty pounds in the first two months of riding.

What had been restless nights since the time I had started drinking suddenly became restful as the stress that used to harass me all night long burned away during my rides to work.

One day, a woman I worked with who commuted fifty miles from New York to New Jersey each day, saw me getting on my bike and getting ready to ride home. She said, "I wish I could ride to work every day. You're really lucky."

As I rode home that afternoon, the headlamp on my bike flickering along the sidewalk in the now dusky fall evening, I started laughing at myself. I had spent so many mornings feeling sorry for myself, telling myself that working the program had been such a total waste of time, and here was someone who, getting into her car for the fifty mile commute through brutal North Jersey traffic, looked at me and my bike and thought, "Boy, that guy is really lucky. He gets to ride his bike to work."

It brought it all home to me. What I saw as a negative, others saw as a positive. Riding the bike to work wasn't a good or bad thing in and of itself; it was what I decided to make of it. My punishment had, in fact, become something of a blessing, just as I'd been told it would—as long as I worked my program.

I wish I could say that from that point on I enjoyed total serenity and acceptance, but the program doesn't work that way for me. I am new and still have my ups and downs, days when I lose faith and take my will back. I make sure to share when I am feeling frustrated or down at meetings because I want the guys with less time than me to know that sobriety isn't a blissed-out fantasy life where we never suffer or doubt.

But I also like to share about the positives that have happened for me during my time in the program, especially how one time when I gave myself lemons through my drunk driving, the program made them into lemonade—despite me.

*Richard D.*
*Red Bank, New Jersey*
*August 2004*

## Alcoholics Anonymous

AA's program of recovery is fully set forth in its basic text, *Alcoholics Anonymous* (commonly known as the Big Book), now in its Fourth Edition, as well as in *Twelve Steps and Twelve Traditions, Living Sober,* and other books. Information on AA can also be found on AA's website at www.aa.org, or by writing to: Alcoholics Anonymous, Box 459, Grand Central Station, New York, NY 10163. For local resources, check your local telephone directory under "Alcoholics Anonymous." Four pamphlets, "This is A.A.," "Is A.A. For You?," "44 Questions," and "A Newcomer Asks" are also available from AA.

## The AA Grapevine

The Grapevine is AA's international monthly journal, published continuously since its first issue in June 1944. The AA pamphlet on the Grapevine describes its scope and purpose this way: "As an integral part of Alcoholics Anonymous for more than sixty years, the Grapevine publishes articles that reflect the full diversity of experience and thought found within the AA fellowship. No one viewpoint or philosophy dominates its pages, and in determining content, the editorial staff relies on the principles of the Twelve Traditions."

In addition to a monthly magazine, the Grapevine also produces anthologies, audiobooks, and CDs based on published articles, an annual wall calendar, and a pocket planner. The entire collection of Grapevine articles is available online in its Digital Archive. AudioGrapevine, the magazine in digital audio format, is available as well. AA Grapevine also publishes La Viña, AA's Spanish-language magazine.

For more information on the Grapevine, or to subscribe, please visit the magazine's website at www.aagrapevine.org or write to:

**The AA Grapevine**
475 Riverside Drive, New York, NY 10115
You may also call:  1-800-631-6025 (US)
1-386-246-0149 (International)